So You Wa... Open a Restaurant!

A Simple, Step by Step Process for Opening and Running Your Own Restaurant

Tom Wilscam

Strategic Book Group

Strategic Book Group
P.O. Box 333
Durham CT 06422
www.StrategicBookClub.com

ISBN: 978-1-60911-980-5

Page composition by J. K. Eckert & Co., Inc.

Printed in the United States of America

Contents

Foreword

The process of opening a restaurant from start to finish can be, and should be, an arduous one. It requires a tremendous amount of research and determination, and it can easily get overwhelming. I am often asked by clients, "What should I be doing?" It's the right question, but not easily answered. Why? Because there is a whole array of things that must be done simultaneously in opening any business, but especially one as complex as a restaurant. One overwhelmed client came to me and, totally exasperated, exclaimed to be lost in the process and didn't know how to proceed. I provided them the following flow chart to help visualize the process in linear form. They told me that it really helped them refocus.

After you take a look at the How to Open a Restaurant Flowchart, I hope you'll enjoy my story as you keep in mind the process from start to finish as illustrated. My goal is to enlighten you about the joys and challenges of the restaurant business and the importance of setting up "systems that run the restaurant, so you and your managers can run the systems." If you can grasp this concept and successfully open your restaurant, you will avoid the burn-out so commonly seen in the restaurant industry. With established systems, you will not have to muscle your business day after day, and you can embrace the joys of restaurant ownership that include making a reasonable profit while enjoying the pride of providing your customers a quality dining experience.

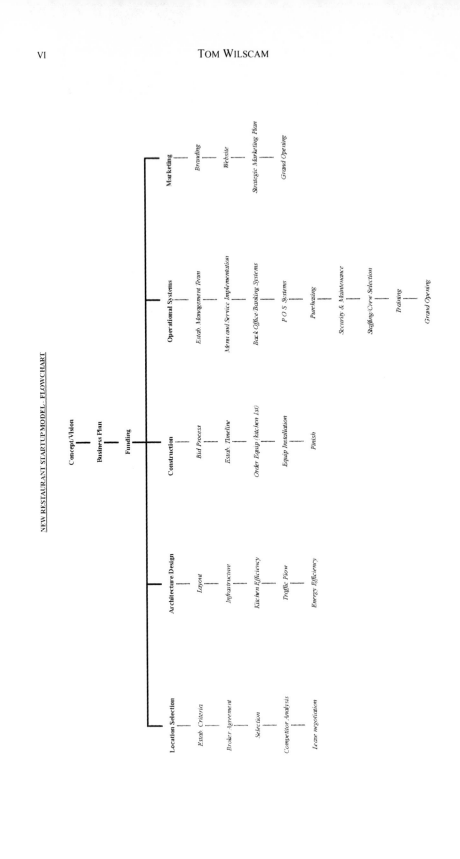

NEW RESTAURANT STARTUP MODEL - FLOWCHART

Concept/Vision

Business Plan

Funding

Location Selection

Estab. Criteria

Broker Agreement

Selection

Competitor Analysis

Lease negotiation

Architecture Design

Layout

Infrastructure

Kitchen Efficiency

Traffic Flow

Energy Efficiency

Construction

Bid Process

Estab. Timeline

Order Equip (kitchen 1st)

Equip Installation

Finish

Operational Systems

Estab. Management Team

Menu and Service Implementation

Back Office Banking Systems

P O S Systems

Purchasing

Security & Maintenance

Staffing/Crew Selection

Training

Grand Opening

Marketing

Branding

Website

Strategic Marketing Plan

Grand Opening

Acknowledgments

There are many who have contributed greatly to my success in the restaurant industry, and I am proud of the small part that I may have had in their successes.

Let me name a few of the most significant:

Fred Mikawa: I met Fred at the University of Colorado. He was an apprentice architect when he designed my first restaurant, the Hungry Farmer. He later became a significant part of Wilscam Enterprises, where he established and ran our restaurant design division, WE II. In addition to the first Hungry Farmer, he designed the Boulder and Colorado Springs' Hungry Farmers, the Hungry Dutchman, Broker, No 3 Lift, PTI restaurants in Denver, Dallas, Houston, Atlanta, Cleveland, and Austin. He also designed several of the most prominent restaurants and clubs in Denver. Fred now lives in Hawaii and is a renowned architect for a number of international resorts.

John Cowan: John began as a waiter in one of my restaurants while still a student, and later became my company's financial VP. He was an important member of my Board of Directors, and I relied on his judgment and expertise a great deal. John now has his own media consulting service, and is quite successful.

The Samaras Brothers: George Samaras was the chef at the first Hungry Farmer. His older brother was the head bartender, and his younger brother the bus person. George and his brothers later went on to own and operate his own restaurants.

Era Trigs: Era was the chef at the original Hungry Farmer for a time. Era taught me how to cook when I graduated from washing potatoes at the Alpine Inn restaurant. Later, she was instrumental in the success of the Hungry Dutchman as its executive chef.

Ed Novak: Ed began his restaurant career with me as an assistant manager at the Hungry Farmer in Boulder. Ed eventually bought the Broker from the company and turned it into one of the most successful restaurants in Denver. Ed has gone on to own and operate many of Denver's best restaurants. His restaurant empire continues to grow at this writing.

Fred Borra: Fred was a chef at the Boulder Hungry Farmer, and later ran the Monfort Meat Packing commissary that my company managed. Fred later partnered with Ed Novak, and his expertise was a major factor in Ed's company's growth. Fred and his wife Carol now own and operate a restaurant in Colorado.

Dan Wolfson: Dan first came to work for me as a dishwasher at the Hungry Dutchman when he was fifteen years old. (I think that he may have lied about his age.) Over the years and while attending the University of Denver, Dan progressed through the kitchen, front of the house positions, and eventually to management. Dan has been an entrepreneur, starting several different businesses. Dan and I once owned a restaurant together and now own and operate a national restaurant consulting company together.

Reid Pasko: I first met Reid when my wife and I were newly married. We were living in the same apartment complex. Reid, at the time, was working as a salesman for Carnation Cream. I offered him a job, and it turned out to be one of my better decisions. Reid worked for me for approximately ten years, and then went on to open the Briar Wood Inn in Golden, Colorado. The Briar Wood Inn has enjoyed a reputation as one of the best restaurants in Colorado for the past thirty years. Reid recently passed away and he will be missed.

Roy Van Dyke: Roy was a restaurant equipment salesman for a local company. We started a restaurant equipment division of Wilscam Enterprises, WE III, that Roy headed up. Fred Mikawa would design the restaurants and Roy would equip them. Roy now owns and runs a successful business as a manufacturer's representative.

Section I:
Introduction

It sounds like a great business to be in, looks fairly easy to learn, and what's classier than being called a *restaurateur?* If you're like most aspiring restaurateurs, you probably think the first step in learning the business is to copy a successful restaurant and then throw in a few innovations of your own to put your stamp on it and make it even better. So what's the big deal? For starters, it's not as easy as you might think.

This book is based on my nearly fifty years in the restaurant business as an owner and operator. Much of what I learned was a direct result of my mistakes; and most of those were from lack of restaurant experience and/or knowledge of the industry.

A few years back, the National Restaurant Association published a report on the ratio of successes to failures in the restaurant business. As you may have guessed, the restaurant business has one of the highest failure rates among all business enterprises in the country. But here's the big surprise: the NRA report stated that 86% of the people who purchased a successful restaurant franchise flourished, while 82% of those who went into the business with no experience or professional industry help failed within the first year of operation.

Why the disparity? Simple—those who purchased a successful franchise were buying a proven system for success. In other words, the franchisor had made mistakes, learned from them, and was then able to pass on their "secrets to success" to the new franchisees!

Those who failed, the aspiring but inexperienced would-be entrepreneurs, were simply not aware of the specific rules and guidelines they needed to be successful. Running a restaurant can seem deceivingly simple to a non-professional because so much of it is based on what you cannot see or experience as a customer. Here's a perfect example:

Site selection: Proper site selection is more detailed and complex than you might imagine, but it's an important key to success in the business. Prospective franchisees often tell me, "I have a great location in mind for a restaurant." When I ask "Okay, why is it so great?" they invariably answer, "It's only a few blocks from where I live." I guarantee this is not one of the criteria for selecting the right location, and more than likely will lead to financial disaster.

Buy a franchise: There are few similarities between restaurants and other retail businesses. Therefore, if you have never owned or managed a restaurant, buying a franchise, where the operating details already exist, is a great way to start. However, even with the proven systems provided by a franchise, there are significant disadvantages to buying a franchise. You will pay a front-end licensing agreement fee, typically from $25,000 to $50,000. Also, as part of the franchise agreement, you will pay 5% to 8% of your gross sales as an ongoing royalty. Additionally, there will be a marketing fund contribution, normally 2%. These fees, based on your gross sales, can easily amount to 40% to 50% of your net profit. Finally, you will have no freedom to change any aspect of your restaurant that you feel would make it more appealing to your specific local trade market.

The best alternative to owning your own restaurant is to first gain the necessary experience by working for a successful restaurant. However, if you're convinced you can make a go of it creating your own restaurant, without a franchise or personal restaurant experience, with a unique, *can't miss* concept, first read this book. I guarantee it will give you a better understanding of why most new restaurants fail, why the smart entrepreneurs succeed, and the pitfalls you should avoid.

The goal of this book is to make you aware of how much you don't know about the restaurant business; and then share with you the knowledge that was instrumental to my success. I hope my years of experience can help make your dream come true and help you avoid the mistakes that the 82% made who were eager to get their restaurants up and running, and then failed. I'll show you how to open your dream restaurant and how to avoid the mistakes that often lead to failure.

When I talk about success, I mean financial success. Owning your own restaurant can be personally rewarding in many ways but, if you are not financially successful, all the ego satisfaction in the world doesn't amount to a hill of beans when your restaurant fails.

A few years back, I was asked to teach a class at the University of Denver Hotel and Restaurant Management School. The class was on Entrepreneurialism, and was offered as an elective for graduate students. It would be offered for one semester only. I was intrigued by the challenge, and accepted. Thirty-two grad students signed up and I began to feel intimidated: I had only been an average student in school, more into sports than trig and ancient history, and I wondered if I was up to the level of the students in my class. I then realized they had signed up for a course they knew nothing about, but one in which I had a ton of experience. That's why they were there—to learn from me. Once I realized this, the rest was easy.

The first day of class, I let the class know that they would receive an *A* or an *F* only: an *A* if they completed the project that I had in mind and an *F* if they did not. They would be graded on this one project alone.

My introductory lecture consisted of the story of my first restaurant management job. I told them that the story would be pertinent to the class project, so they needed to listen up. Here it is, as I best remember it:

In 1959, I enrolled at the University of Colorado. I was there on a football scholarship after two years at the University of Southern California and a stint in the military. In the off-season and summer vacations while at CU, I supported myself by working part-time as a waiter. This seemed to be the perfect part-time job for a college student. Flexible hours, minimal experience required, and good money for the effort put forward. Additionally, I found that I enjoyed the interaction with the customers.

Looking back, I now realize that there might have been a trend taking place; I had started working in restaurants when I was fourteen years old, as a soda jerk at a little restaurant across from my high school. I thought it great fun to create the spectacular ice cream sundaes and sodas that were offered. Also, as a side benefit, I did my share of sampling.

Though my high school and college years of working in restaurants had given me a feel for the food industry, my football experience in those years was significant because it taught me how relevant participating in a team sport would be to my success as a restaurant manager, and later to owning my first restaurant. Why? Team sports—the successful working together as a team with others who excel at their positions—teaches you to acquire those management skills of team work that are imperative if you want to be a successful restaurateur.

During my senior year at CU, I worked in a restaurant called the Terrace Inn, located just outside of Boulder, Colorado. After finishing college, and while waiting for a response to the many resumes I sent out, I continued to work at the Terrace Inn. One day, the owner approached me, knowing I was out of school, and inquired if I would care to manage the restaurant! (*Is he playing with a full deck?* I asked myself). I reminded him that I had *no* management experience and zilch knowledge of how to run a restaurant. Because I was older, due to my two years in the service, he felt I would do fine. To put it another way, since the restaurant was not doing well, he probably figured I couldn't make things much worse. One difficulty was the *location.* The restaurant was located between two small towns, Boulder and Golden, with few businesses or significant residential density in the area. Second, the food would never win any culinary awards.

Having nothing to lose and, luckily, having excellent contacts, I came up with the following idea: Having played football at CU and knowing personally most of the athletes in varsity sports, it was easy to approach the well-known stars in each sport. First on my list was a football teammate who was also a two-time All-American. Next, I approached the All Conference CU quarterback, and then another All-American teammate who just happened to be the number one NFL draft pick the following year. Additionally, I recruited another football star who had won an Olympic medal, and rounded out my list with the best-known basketball, track, and baseball players I could think of. I told them my plan, and they all agreed to give it a try.

The athletes became my wait staff at the Terrace Inn. On each of the tables they would be serving, I placed a tent card with a short bio on them and their athletic careers. Before long, the word got out around the campus and the city of Boulder. Within weeks, we had lines out the door and halfway down the block. And, though the food and service would have a tough time winning an Award of Excellence, we had a gimmick that worked! Just imagine if the cuisine was Five-Star and my waiters, in addition to their athletic accomplishments, knew what they were doing! We would have earned an entry in the *Guide Michelin.* Anyway, we had a great time, made some money for the owner and ourselves, and the experience gave me some solid ideas for a career path.

The funny thing about this whole experiment and the increase in the restaurant's business was that, now, the only thing that was worse than the food was the service.

Don't think that because one lucky idea worked I was now a qualified restaurant manager. The unpredictable frequently happens in the restaurant business, so you must be constantly on your toes. One day at lunch, a Terrace Inn customer approached me with plate in hand and fire in his eyes. He thrust the sandwich on his plate in my face and then lifted the top slice of bread to reveal a cigarette butt planted firmly on his ham and cheese. What I learned from that lesson was that *cooks are not allowed to smoke in the kitchen!* Apparently, the cook had placed his cigarette on the shelf above the sandwich line and it fell onto the sandwich. At least that was a better thought than the alternative—that the cook had done it on purpose.

Another anecdote in the *what not to do* manual in the restaurant business is taken from a book called *My Secret Life on the McJob,* by Jerry Newman. He and his daughter had lunch at a national chain restaurant. Each had ordered a hamburger plate with fries and all the trimmings. Upon her first bite, his daughter discovered a foreign object in her burger. Her father, to his horror, thought it was a condom! At this point, the mortified store manager stepped in, looked the offending object over carefully, and convinced his customers it was really the finger of a rubber glove, and not to worry. I doubt if Mr. Newman and his family ever returned there for another meal. It made little difference that the local health department of virtually every state requires that rubber or latex gloves be worn by all restaurant food handlers. Now how do you suppose that a rubber glove finger found its way onto that girl's hamburger plate? My guess is that a kitchen employee, with a misplaced sense of humor or plain boredom, put it there. Still think you want to own a restaurant?

Another painful memory from those days at the Terrace Inn should be proof positive that if I could become successful in the restaurant business, anyone could. During my senior year at CU, one of my roommates, and my teammate on the football team, was a young man named Denny Krueger. Denny was one of those fortunate sons whose father was supportive of everything Denny did. His dad attended most team practices and, I'm sure, never missed a game during Denny's career. His dad, Carl Krueger, had been mayor of Cody, Wyoming, where Denny grew up. During the years of my close friendship with Denny, I became very fond of Carl and, I think, he of me.

After graduation, Denny took time off to enjoy the good life before the inevitable settling down. After several months of ski bumming, Denny came back to Boulder to apply for law school. One day, he and his dad dropped by the Terrace Inn to say hello. When they entered the restaurant, I happened to be carrying a large tray of food for a table of six. In my enthusiasm at seeing them, I lost my concentration, then my balance. The thing that flashed in my mind was where to dump the tray. I had two options: either to dump it on a nearby table of four beautifully groomed ladies, splattering them with food, or slamming the tray against the nearest wall. I chose the wall. My next dilemma was whether to stand there gripping the tray against the wall, trying to assume a casual look of "doesn't everyone do this," or just let it go.

When I saw the startled expressions on the faces of Denny and Carl, who were rooted to the spot as if watching a ten-car pile-up on a freeway, we all broke up with laughter and, with embarrassment and resignation; I surrendered to the inevitable and let the tray go clattering to the floor.

I began cleaning up the mess, made a humble apology to the four ladies for the near disaster, and wondered what was going through Carl and Denny's minds: "Tom, maybe you and the restaurant business aren't a match made in heaven."

After I told the class my Terrace Inn story (hoping they weren't scared off), I let them know what the semester project would be. They were to write a business plan on how to start a new restaurant and how to make it a success. I related my Terrace Inn experiences to encourage them to be creative and think outside the box in writing their business plan, and to be flexible and ready for anything in a business where anything can happen (we're all human), but where chefs, the maitre d,' and the wait staff must come together in harmony to create the perfect dining experience for the customer.

Remember, these were hotel/restaurant graduate students, so they should have already acquired a smattering of book knowledge on where to start and where to go to complete their projects. However, being college students, they would most likely be somewhat structured and perhaps overly academic. I wanted them to be creative and, as I said, to think outside the box.

"Being creative means finding a solution outside the normal framework of thinking. Let's take a paper clip. We all know it's made for one primary purpose—to hold papers together. Yet,

putting your creative juices to work, what other purposes might we find for the paper clip? Fish hook...finger nail cleaner...key ring...a way to fix your glasses...a tool to pick a lock, or a pin to stick a note on a message board? All of us possess a spark of creativity within us. It's available anytime, for any situation.

—*Persistence: The Art of Failing Until You Succeed,* Ernie Carwile

How creative were my students? Well, I still keep many of their business plans and enjoy reviewing them when I want to reminisce about the pleasures of teaching that class. The class met once a week for two hours, during which we would discuss each step of creating a comprehensive business plan that would help them realize their dreams of opening their own restaurant. Since much of this book will deal with how to best open your dream restaurant, let's begin as I did:

It is the first day out of school. You have no management restaurant experience, no money, no concept in mind, and no location. You only possess a burning desire to become a successful restaurant entrepreneur. So, where do you start? With a plan, of course. Without one, it's like shooting from the hip. Just trusting your instincts is a recipe for failure. "If you don't know where you're going, you are unlikely to get anywhere worthwhile." So you begin with a business plan, a proven foundation of success and the road map to your dream becoming reality. A quotation worth remembering and putting into practice is, *"Failing to plan is planning to fail"* (*The 7 Habits of Highly Effective People,* Stephen R. Covey).

Let's outline two important steps necessary to create a successful business plan:

1. You must have an idea of the type of restaurant you want. That means coming up with a well-thought-out concept, visualizing it with graphics, and describing in writing. Your entire business plan will evolve from this: how to bring that dream restaurant to life; how to give it its unique personality; and what makes it different from other restaurants.

2. Study successful restaurants in order to formulate a model that fits what you have in mind. You don't have to copy them, just determine why you think they are successful. Is it their food? Is it their friendly service or atmosphere? Most likely it will be all three, fitting together to form a total concept: great food, prompt and attentive service, and a comfortable, if not unique, atmosphere.

I like to use the example of a three-legged milking stool to drive this point home. If one leg is weak, then the whole stool is weak and collapses, hopefully not with you on it.

In my case, I selected what I felt was, at that time, the best restaurant in Denver to emulate. My idea was not necessarily to copy the elements of its success, but to learn from it. The restaurant was called the Alpine Village Inn. The décor was authentic, old country German; the wait staff was dressed in traditional leather lederhosen, and the menu and service decidedly German. The Alpine Village Inn epitomized the successful three-legged stool model: great food, fabulous service, and a fun and authentic atmosphere.

When I suggest learning from observing other successful restaurants, keep this thought in mind. Your restaurant idea must be uniquely yours. Combine the best parts of other successful restaurants into your own creative version of what you want. Perhaps it's the personal service and unique food presentation that you have enjoyed at one restaurant, or the décor theme at another. Blend all the elements that you feel make those restaurants successful into your own total concept of food, atmosphere, and service, and you will have created your own original.

MY EDUCATION BEGINS

The only thing I knew for sure at this time was that I didn't know what I didn't know, so I had better figure out a way to learn what I didn't know.

My education began when I introduced myself to the owner of the Alpine Village Inn in Denver. His name was Ray Dambaugh, a man about sixty-five years old, with a history of successes in the restaurant industry. I told Mr. Dambaugh of my desire to learn the business and to eventually open my own restaurant. I asked him for a job so that I could learn from him. What I saw in the Alpine Village Inn was a total restaurant concept carried out in every respect.

In my naivety, I also told Mr. Dambaugh that I wanted to learn from him so that I could open a restaurant just like his. Mr. Dambaugh—to no surprise—was less enthusiastic about teaching me the restaurant business than I was about learning it. He told me that he currently had no job openings.

Being determined, I told him that I would work for nothing if he would teach me the business. I'm sure that he doubted my sincerity as well as my sanity, and figured that I would not last very long. However, free labor was free labor—for however long. Mr. Dambaugh informed me that a successful restaurant begins with the food, therefore, I should begin my learning process in the kitchen. He was right, of course—the kitchen is the foundation of any restaurant; but I think that he initially carried it a little too far. For the first two weeks, eight hours a day, I did nothing but wash potatoes and perform kitchen cleanup work. This was, I'm sure, Ray's way of testing me to see if I was really sincere about my offer to work for free, and to determine if I had the tenacity to stick it out.

Needing the money, I took a job in the mornings as a laborer with a construction company. The company, owned by a CU football booster I knew, was sympathetic to my dream and allowed me to work part-time. I would begin at seven A.M. and work until noon. At one P.M., I reported to my job in the kitchen at the Alpine Village Inn. After two weeks of washing potatoes and cleaning up the kitchen, I began to wonder if perhaps I might be overqualified for the job. Was this all there was to the restaurant business?

About that time, I believe Ray began to realize that I was serious and perhaps began to feel a little guilty. He promoted me from potatoes to food preparation, where I learned to cut meat, make soups from scratch, and prepare the basic ingredients for the Alpine's German menu.

Next, I was moved to third line cook, then eventually to second line cook. Then, for a short time while the chef was on vacation, I ran the kitchen. Somehow, thankfully, the restaurant survived this brief period. Ray continued to take an apparent and growing interest in me. After my shift each evening, he would take me to his office in the back of the restaurant and spend an hour or two explaining the financial aspects of running a restaurant: how to calculate and control food and labor costs. I learned how to order and control inventory, as well as the many other basics of cost control. Since Ray had racked up nearly forty-five years of restaurant experience, he also included some of the more subtle aspects of financial management in this business, which owner/operators pick up over time.

In addition to the back-of-the-house (kitchen) training, I spent time bartending and running the dining room staff. During my apprenticeship with Ray, which lasted approximately nine months, Ray honored our agreement and I was never paid a nickel. In return, I received free meals (the food was exceptional) and, most important of all, I learned the fundamentals of how to run a successful restaurant.

One day, Ray asked me to take a ride with him. He showed me a restaurant location that was no longer in business. He said he had an opportunity to lease the space and asked me if I would be interested in running it under his direction. The restaurant was large and built in the style of a log cabin. With steadfast focus on the three-legged stool concept, he named the restaurant the North Woods Inn. The theme would be built around the mythical North Woods character, Paul Bunyan, with the atmosphere decidedly rustic. The food would be wholesome and delicious, with generous portions served family style. Waiters and waitresses would dress to look like authentic North Woods folks—loggers and calico-wardrobed ladies.

Because of Ray's innovative brilliance—his ability to make the three legs of the stool work together in harmony—the North Woods Inn was a huge success. After two years of managing the North Woods Inn under Ray's tutelage, I decided it was time to venture out on my own. Ray had been paying me a generous salary, plus 20% of the profits each quarter as a bonus. When I told Ray of my decision to leave, and about my restaurant idea, he wished me luck and paid me a fair value for the 20% as if I were part owner, regarding the money as more than a bonus.

Ray is gone now, but I am eternally grateful to him for his generosity, his teaching, and the opportunities that he provided for me to learn. The saying that "he taught me everything I know" truly applies to Ray Dambaugh.

I am often asked the question, "What is the most important thing to achieve success in the restaurant business? Is it experience? Is it location? Is it financial acumen? Is it luck?" My answer is always the same. "All those elements are important, certainly, but the most important quality for success is personal tenacity." In other words, if you can't get it done one way, keep trying until you find a way that works. Then stick to it.

> *"I do not believe it possible to succeed at anything without a certain amount of tenacity. In fact, the greater one's tenacity, the greater one's success. There are many examples of how apparent failure turns into success. Normally we hear mostly about the success part and not the failures. Thomas Edison had over 900 failures in his efforts to produce an electric light. Henry Ford went bankrupt twice during his first three years in business. Dr. Seuss was rejected by twenty-three publishers before he succeeded in selling over six million copies of his*

first children's book. The best baseball teams lose fifty to sixty games a year, and of course there is Abe Lincoln, who lost more elections than anyone else before becoming one of our country's greatest men.

—*Persistence: The Art of Failing Until You Succeed,* Ernie Carwile

"It isn't whether you get knocked down; it's whether you get back up."

—Vince Lombardi.

You have no idea how applicable Coach Lombardi's quote was to my career as a football player at University of Colorado and, later, to my life career as an owner/operator of many successful restaurants and restaurant chains. I learned quickly that getting knocked down goes with the territory, but the most important thing of all is to get back up again...and again...and again. As I see it, the only difference between the winners and losers in the game of life is that the winners keep getting back up.

Now a word about motivation. Motivation, to me, is the spark plug that starts the motor. With motivation comes the incentive you need to pursue your dream. However, motivation without tenacity is like starting the motor but not putting the car in gear. So, just as motivation is the spark plug that gets you started, tenacity, sticking to your goal fiercely, is the motor that gets you there. More about motivation later.

GETTING STARTED

With tenacity as a given, the next step is to come up with the right concept for your restaurant. Several factors must be considered: First, you must think of your restaurant as a *product to be sold.* That leads automatically to the next question: what product will appeal to the most people in the area where you plan to open? The economy of the area—what your customers are willing to pay for good food and service—will determine the price point (median pricing) of your menu.

Certainly, the economy in the chosen area should play a part in the decision of your concept. During tough economic times, people will still eat out. However, the more expensive white tablecloth, full service restaurants will suffer the most. The general public more often will tend to make their restaurant choices based on its price points.

Next, the lifestyle of the majority of people in the area is critical. Are you in a rural or an urban environment? The geographic area of the country should influence your concept and menu decisions. A concept that may work in the south may not work as well in the north. A western cowboy or California surfer motif may not work in a blue collar, industrial area. A concept geared to an urban office environment may not work in an urban residential area. A concept that seems a natural in an urban college town may go down in flames in a rural area.

The demographics of an area are extremely important and are a major influence in determining the right location for your restaurant. As you outline the requirements for your dream restaurant, consider this example, from my own experience.

My location choice for starting my first restaurant was Denver, Colorado. I lived there, and knew the city and the market intimately. The time was the early 1960s, and Denver was a strong, family-oriented city, with a Midwestern lifestyle. Having a feel for its personality and values, I zeroed in on the Alpine Village Inn and the North Woods Inn, two of the most successful restaurants in Denver. With their friendly, unpretentious atmosphere and mid-level price range, they became the models on which I would base my first restaurant. Most importantly, I felt their success was due to their emphasis on theme. Very few restaurants in Denver at that time had a theme that carried out the three-legged stool concept as well as they did.

For my theme, I envisioned a farm setting of food, service and atmosphere, which led to choosing the Hungry Farmer as my restaurant's name. The menu reflected that concept: what would a typical farm family have for dinner, and how would it be served? Homemade, country fried chicken was a natural and became a popular staple of the menu. Fresh Colorado trout, a Rocky Mountain specialty, was another natural. Following in quick order were hearty T-bone steak, roast duck, pan-fried catfish, and beef steak pot pie.

The remaining entrees fell into place: spare ribs, old fashioned pot roast, calves' liver & onions, and, for the more adventurous palates, Rocky Mountain oysters. I didn't know if mountain oysters would go over, but I did know they would create good-humored conversation in the dining room. When asked by a customer what they were, our waiters discreetly replied that mountain oysters were the specialty that remained when a bull was persuaded, often against his will, to become a steer. "Okay, we'll…uh…try it."

For a group of twenty or more, I would offer roast suckling pig (local mountain boar), served appropriately, with an apple stuffed in its mouth, carved and served at the table.

Each meal included homemade soup served in a stainless steel custom made milk pail, with homemade oatmeal muffins, corn bread, and cinnamon rolls served in an egg basket. To complement the fresh baked rolls, each table would have a ceramic apple, filled with fresh apple butter. A farm-fresh, tossed greens salad, seasonal fresh vegetables, and choice of potato would accompany the entrées.

Next, I began to envision the atmosphere. As every farm has a house and a barn, so my restaurant would be built in the style of a yellow farm house with red trim window shutters. There would be window flower boxes, a front porch with a swing, and the entrance doors made of wood with ornate, cut-glass windows. Next, a working hay wagon was placed in front of the barn doors.

As they passed through the front door, our dinner guests entered a vestibule, with a colorful, early American rope throw rug on the floor, a large, wooden coat stand, and a vintage dresser with decorative mirror off to one side. After leaving the vestibule, they entered the lounge area with its Midwestern-style bar. Leaving nothing to chance, I decided the bar stools would have authentic metal tractor seats. Although I had never sat on one, I figured they had to be comfortable if a farmer or ranch hand sat on one all day as he plowed the lower forty.

Additionally, I was a great admirer of the innovations that the Trader Vic's chains introduced to their cocktail menu. Vic Bergeron, the man who created these iconic south sea restaurants in the 1940s, had clearly followed the three-legged milking stool concept of food, atmosphere, and service. The atmosphere and menu was Polynesian, with their famous drink menu carrying the Polynesian theme to new heights. Drink offerings like the Mai Tai, Fog Cutter, Navy Grog— plus several other dark and light rum concoctions—became world famous, and were served in equally unique drink containers: ceramic replicas of Polynesian-inspired designs. I was sure that I could do the same thing with ceramic vegetables and fruits, applying the same idea to a Midwestern farm-style drink menu of original concoctions.

From a creative concept session with friends, we developed our version of unique drinks: the Watermelon Whoopee, served for two in a large ceramic half watermelon with two long straws; the Cantaloupe Eloper for two, served in a half-ceramic cantaloupe; the Corn in the Cob, a cocktail served in a ceramic ear of corn, and the Apple-Pie-

Eyed—you guessed it—served in a ceramic apple. I had found a ceramic shop that would make these and other ceramic drink containers that fit my concept.

This creative concept session, which convened at my apartment to create the above names and corresponding drink recipes, had an upside and a downside. You understand, of course, that the only sure way to create an original drink with a killer reputation is to taste and evaluate it as you develop it. These *roll back prohibition* sessions made for a fun evening, but not a fun morning.

For lounge entertainment, the idea of a giant copper still on stage intrigued me. A large glass gauge with a red Danger Warning line would be clearly visible and, when the gauge reached the danger zone, the still would begin to shake and vent steam. This would happen every twenty to thirty minutes. When the restaurant became a reality, the still always caused a stir with the bar patrons, who looked nervously over their shoulders, refreshments suspended in air, holding on to their drinks for dear life.

Musical entertainment was a must, so we rolled out an old-fashioned upright piano on stage. The strings were exposed and wired with colored lights to keep beat with the key pads when struck by the piano player. A banjo player or two accompanied our pianist and, during breaks, we showed the classic silent movies of Mack Sennett, the Keystone Kops, and the beloved little tramp, Charlie Chaplin. What's a good movie without popcorn? To answer that need, voila; we brought out an old-fashioned popcorn wagon that popped fresh popcorn, which you could drench with hot butter from a dispenser.

The adjacent barn was the actual dining area. Of course, any barn would have a hay loft, so we scattered imitation hay bales around, with stuffed hens and geese perched on top of the hay bales. Old, iron, pot-bellied stoves were placed in the dining room and all manner of farm artifacts decorated the dining room walls. The tables were covered with red, green, and yellow checkered tablecloths and the table lamps were actually ceramic cider jugs with candles and inverted copper funnel shades. The waiters were dressed in bib overalls with straw hats, and the waitresses decked out in gaily colored, milkmaid costumes, complete with pantaloon bloomers and bonnets.

The Hungry Farmer brings back some wonderful memories. It was my first successful venture as an owner in the restaurant business, with some classic stories attached to it: like the night the Shriners came to town. The national Shriners convention was held in Denver that year and approximately fifty Shriners showed up for dinner one

Saturday night. Apparently, one of the Shriners owned a Chevrolet car dealership, because his buddies all arrived in twenty-five identical, red, Corvette convertibles. Our parking lot looked like a Corvette dealership. Shriners like to party during their annual conventions, and this group of fifty was no exception. They were well-behaved, considering this was a major boys' night out, and they thoroughly enjoyed their evening of good food and entertainment.

After they left, I thought all had gone well until a customer walked in and asked if I had sold the old wagon that used to be in front of the barn. I was confused by the question. "It's still there," I replied. He then said he could swear he had just passed my wagon on the street, drawn behind a red Corvette. I jumped into my car, pursued and caught the Corvette, spoke a few gentle words with the Shriner, and retrieved my wagon.

Another memorable incident, one that may cast some doubt on my good judgment in those early days of my career took place at the second Hungry Farmer in Boulder. The time was the mid-sixties, when the Beatles, the Rolling Stones, and Janis Joplin were the reigning rock icons. The University of Colorado in Boulder, like many state universities of that era, had a strong liberal bent, with a large number of students part of the hippie culture. The hippies had their own dress code that, at times, excluded a shirt, shoes, and socks.

Being a family restaurant, I felt that our regular customers might find it offensive to be sitting next to someone shirtless and in bare feet. We therefore mandated a dress policy of shirt and shoes. One evening, a couple of bare-chested and barefoot students were turned away because of the dress code. I received a call at home from the store manager who told me what had happened, and that the two characters had returned. However, they were not alone. They were with twenty of their friends, all dressed (or undressed) in the same manner, and now sitting on the floor, blocking the entrance to the dining room. The manager wanted to know what to do. I told him to do nothing until I arrived.

When I arrived at the restaurant, I made an ill-advised executive decision. I assumed that even hippies pursuing an education would observe the logic of a brilliant compromise—simply go back to the dorm, put on a shirt and shoes (if they indeed owned any), and then they could eat. Unfortunately, that logic had been offered by the restaurant manager, to no avail.

Entering the restaurant through the kitchen, I told the manager to gather all the male cooks and waiters and meet me on the front lawn. I then walked around the restaurant and entered by the front door.

The leader of the group sat at the front with his friends, squatting on the floor in the classic sit-in posture of the period. He had long blond hair tied into a pony tail. Proceeding with my executive decision, I confronted him; before anyone realized what was happening, I had grabbed the leader by his pony tail and was out the front door in a flash, dragging him behind me.

You can imagine what followed. When his shirtless cohort followed us out to the front lawn, my male staff, with some trepidation, awaited them. When it looked like we were all about to mimic the restaurant's famed giant still with the Warning Danger red line, the police arrived in the nick of time and broke up what had all the elements of turning into a full scale brawl. At that point, the officer in charge made his own executive decision and we all spent the night in the Boulder jail.

The Boulder police placed all the combatants together in the drunk tank. After a few hours of glaring across the cell block at one another, we began talking, and by the end of the night, we had become friends. Both the hippies and the restaurant had stuck to their respective principles, and we developed a mutual respect. The following morning, I paid the bail for everyone. No charges were filed by either side, and that was the end of it (except for my wife's wrath for my brilliant decision making).

It had a nice ending, however; most of our new hippie friends returned often to the restaurant, always wearing shirt and shoes. There's something to be said for respecting one another's views…even if you don't agree with them.

THE NEXT STEPS

With the Hungry Farmer, I now had my restaurant concept. The next step in my business plan would be a location whose demographics fit my concept. It seemed logical that I should seek out a family oriented, high density office and residential neighborhood for my restaurant. I would need a high density of office and retail within a one-mile radius of the restaurant to support lunch. For dinner, I would need a fairly large residential community within a three-mile radius. With the help of a good commercial realtor, finding the right market area and location for my restaurant was the easy part.

The more difficult part would be to raise the money for the project—the money I had received from Ray for 20% of the North Woods Inn sale was being used for living expenses while I pursued the initial steps of my business plan. I had no family resources to borrow from, and no personal equity to draw on for a bank credit line. I would have to finance my dream in a more creative and perhaps non-traditional way. In other words, I began to think outside the box.

While I attended the University of Colorado, I had become friends with many members of the alumni football booster club. Most of them were successful business men whom I would contact for financial help. Realistically, I knew that to attract anyone to invest in my venture I would need a buttoned-up business plan, complete with sales projections, and showing a solid return on investment.

Following the advice of my lawyer, I selected a Limited Partnership arrangement. This way, investors would have no liability other than the cash they invested. As the General Partner, I would be responsible for all the company's liabilities. However, on a more positive note, as the General Partner, I would also have complete control of operational and business decisions.

In order to make the investment attractive, I would have to sell investors on my restaurant concept, the value of my recently acquired management experience, and that I would pursue an aggressive return on all investments. My plan consisted of the following: the investors would put up 100% of the needed cash and, in return, receive 80% of the equity. I would initially have a 20% founder's stock. The investors' financial return was based on a time factor for doubling their money. They would receive an ongoing payment equal to 15% of their investment after two years, if they had not doubled their initial investment by then. When they had doubled their initial investment, the ownership would then be reversed and I would own 80% and investors would own and receive 20% ownership.

Obviously, there was great incentive on my part to make the Hungry Farmer successful—and as quickly as possible. By hard work and good fortune, I was able to double my investor's money within the first year of the restaurant's operation. Also, because the investors financed 100% of the venture, I had no bank loans to contend with that could have been a road bump on the road to profitability.

There are many other ways to finance your business. By far the easiest is to finance through a traditional lending institution with a possible Small Business Administration (SBA) guarantee. SBA is a government funded department designed to help small business entrepreneurs. With certain requirements, the SBA will guarantee as much as 90% of the bank loan from an SBA authorized bank. The major difficulty here is being able to qualify for the business loan. Typical requirements are that you will need to put up 20% to 25% of the project cost and have one-to-one collateral to cover the 75% to 80% that you are borrowing. In other words, if you are borrowing $400,000, you will need to have $400,000 in solid collateral to secure the loan. However, no matter how strong your collateral may be, a bank will not make the loan nor will the SBA guarantee it unless your business plan makes sense to them.

The way an SBA loan works is that if they are guaranteeing 80% of the loan, you will be required to put up at least 20%, and the bank then has no risk. Obviously, banks will prefer an SBA guarantee unless you have an extremely strong relationship with your bank. The downside to you on an SBA loan is that you will pay additional loan points for it. The upside is that an SBA loan will generally give you a much longer period to amortize your loan with no pre-payment penalties. This can help your monthly cash flow by having a smaller loan payment.

The Hungry Farmer restaurant proved a huge success in the Denver area.

Approximately twenty-four months after opening the first Hungry Farmer, I was ready to open a second restaurant. I had proven to myself and my investors that the three-legged stool of food, atmosphere, and service had worked like a charm in Denver.

A gentleman named John Wagner approached me one day about a plot of land he owned on Interstate 25, well south of metro Denver. At that time, the location was considered to be well on the outskirts of town. John must have been reading my mind because the idea of a destination restaurant had tremendous appeal to me—a new challenge after the success of the Hungry Farmer. The location was no more than a fifteen to twenty minute drive from anywhere in Denver, turning an ordinary night for prospective customers into an adventure—a chance to get out of town while enjoying a great meal. Additionally, John was willing to finance a build-to-suit (he would pay the cost of the building and build it into the rent) on his property for me, which made the total financing package easier.

Because of the success of wholesome family dining that the Hungry Farmer delivered, I decided that a Dutch theme could do the same—be fun and inviting, in a unique environment, while delivering a great meal. The restaurant's name would be the Hungry Dutchman. The building would be in two main sections; the first would be an authentic, five-story, revolving Dutch windmill, visible for miles on I-25, and a landmark that would stand out and be remembered for two decades (how many five-story, working windmills do you see in Colorado?). We would put the lounge and bar on the first two floors of the windmill section. Patrons would then be able to look up from inside and see two gigantic gears driven by the windmill. The gears were connected to a lodge pole with a huge stone mashing wheel that ground wheat or corn—an authentic simulation of a real gristmill. The bar and lounge tables would all be inlaid with colorful Delft tile imported from Holland.

The second section would be the dining room and kitchen, and would be attached to the windmill. At the entrance to the Hungry Dutchman, patrons would cross a wooden bridge with a working waterwheel churning water in a stone moat. Tulips that would bloom in season would be planted throughout the exterior of the building and on either side of a walkway from the parking lot.

My wife and I spent two weeks in Holland researching and collecting items for the décor. We bought two collections of authentic Dutch costumes, one for men and one for women. We visited the town of

Delft, famous for their hand-painted Delft tiles, where we purchased hundreds of them to decorate the bar and lounge area, as well as old artifacts and handmade Dutch wooden boats, wooden shoes, and trinkets for the gift shop.

Three dining rooms rounded out the architectural plan. The first would be done in pastel colors, with Dutch murals on the walls depicting Dutch family life. The second would display a more masculine, nautical theme, using dark woods. Dutch fishing and sailing scenes would adorn the walls and the handmade, wooden Dutch boats that we had purchased in Holland would be placed on shelves on the walls. The third dining room recreated the comfortable and inviting living room of a Dutch home.

The waiters and waitresses would be dressed in authentic costumes designed like the ones we had brought from Holland. They would wear clogs for shoes and the menu would be European and feature a true Dutch delicacy, the famed Dutch split peasoup.

The Dutchman was a huge success. I then opened two more Hungry Farmers, one in Boulder and another in Colorado Springs. Soon after they opened, I took the plunge on another new concept after being approached by three young realtors who had purchased a building in the financial district of downtown Denver. The building they owned was a former bank and had, in the basement, a giant, reinforced steel bank vault. Of course, this gave me all kinds of ideas about the unique atmosphere a restaurant in a bank vault could present. The owners were willing to give me free rent for a period of time if I would put a restaurant in their building. They felt that a good restaurant would help attract tenants.

We named the restaurant the Broker. The décor resembled the Denver downtown financial district of the mid-30s and pictures obtained from the Denver Public Library, depicting that era, would cover the walls. The bank vault itself contained the tables and booths for dining. The menu was more upscale, befitting a financial district clientele. The Broker had a slow start because of its basement location. In the marketing section of this book, you will discover how we managed—with some marketing sleight of hand—to turn that slow start around.

I went on to open many more restaurants, but with these first three concept restaurants, the Hungry Farmers, the Hungry Dutchman, and the Broker, you should now have a basic idea that will stimulate some out of the box ideas for your business plan.

You've made it this far, and I hope I've drawn an accurate picture of the do's and don'ts on the path to opening your dream restaurant. and even entertained you with the fun side of the business. The following sections are a bit drier than *my story,* but will spell out in detail operational systems and procedures that are necessary for financial success.

Section II:
The Business Plan

First, make an outline of what your business plan will include. Remember, BE SPECIFIC! Writing a business plan forces you to think through where you are going, how you plan to get there, and is it a tried and true road map to success? By organizing your thinking, you are more able to translate your thoughts to paper (or a computer screen) and watch a rigorous plan of action begin to take form. If you are going to be successful in business, it is essential to focus on a plan, and retain the principles found in books like *The 7 Habits of Highly Effective People,* by Stephen R. Covey.

Business Plan Table of Contents

- Executive Summary
- The Company Structure
- Restaurant Service Categories
- Service
- Menu
- Customer Profile
- Competition
- Marketing Strategy
- Location
- Ownership
- Management
- Operational Systems
- Financial Requirements
- Interior Floor Plan and Elevation Renderings
- Sales, Profit & Loss Projections

The Executive Summary: Your Executive Summary should be brief and two-fold, containing:

1. A well-thought-out, condensed version of the business plan, that is, the blueprint you use in developing your restaurant concept.
2. The financial plan, which becomes the essential vehicle for securing financing.

The executive summary provides a banker, or potential investor, an insight into your thinking and an implied promise for profits. Condensed and to the point, the executive summary gives your potential investors the essence of the business plan without having to digest the entire document, and creates an immediate interest to read further. Like any novel you're interested in buying, you will probably read the inside cover first for a summarized version of the story line. If the story or subject matter appeals to, you will more likely buy the book. Your business plan, with its executive summary, serves the same purpose. Following is a format of a sample business plan:

The Company Structure: Describe the legal business entity that you have selected to conduct your business as. Your accountant and lawyer will advise you based on your personal circumstances. See Section III: The Nitty Gritty, The Company Structure

Restaurant Service Categories: How will you deliver service to your customers? Are you thinking of table service, with a wait and bus staff, or the limited staff of fast-food or fast-casual service systems? This is an important factor in enhancing your three-legged stool working concept, and will impact your menu pricing structure. Your service concept will determine the qualifications required of the employees you will hire and the pay scale appropriate to each. See Section III: The Nitty Gritty, Restaurant Service Categories.

Service: What *attitude* and personality should your service staff display? How will they interact with your customers? From behind a counter, in a fast food setting, or up close and personal, taking and bringing orders directly to the table with a smile. Good service, plus a pleasant attitude of your wait staff goes a long way in bringing your customers back. See Section III: The Nitty Gritty, Service.

Menu: Write out your menu. Be specific, with a detailed description of each menu item and projected pricing. Explain why you have selected the menu items and how they relate to your service system. Making a Caesar salad tableside does not work in a fast food restaurant. *The menu and your service system are the foundation of your restaurant.* Your thoughtful explanation of why you selected specific menu items will be appreciated by potential investors who need to know you researched your subject thoroughly. See Section III: The Nitty Gritty, Menu.

Customer Profile: In this section, you will describe your target customers, clarifying who your target market potential customers are: their age, sex, income, occupation, marital status. These are all factors to consider in arriving at a profile of the customers who are most likely to patronize your restaurant. Present as clear a profile of your targeted customer as possible, with a sharp eye to demographics. Is your target market white, gray, or blue collar? Write out what you think it is, and then support your supposition with facts to back up how you perceive the demographics. See Section III: The Nitty Gritty, Customer Profile.

Competition: What are the other restaurants in the immediate area of your location? How does your concept for food, service, décor, and atmosphere differ from them? Which types of restaurants are doing the best business? If they're a chain, research their published sales. See Section III: The Nitty Gritty, Competition.

Marketing Strategy: Outline your marketing strategy, point by point. Show how it meshes with your concept. A profile of your target market is essential, especially the specific market within a one- to three-mile radius of your restaurant location. By adopting a hands-on, personalized approach in your marketing efforts, you will avoid the unnecessary expenses of a mass media campaign. See Section III: The Nitty Gritty, Marketing Strategy.

Location, Location, Location: Explain why you chose the location of your restaurant and why you feel it is best-suited to attract customers. Highlight the important demographics of your location, and why the menu, theme, and décor closely match the profile of your target market whom you feel will patronize your restaurant. See Section III: The Nitty Gritty, Location, Location, Location.

Ownership: List the owners/partners of your company and the percentages each will receive. Define what role they will play in the company and include their resumes. A bank will undoubtedly want to see the financial statements of each, and their last two years' tax returns. See Section III: The Nitty Gritty, Ownership.

Management: State in detail what your management strategy will be. Will the principal owner, or owners, function as general manager or will you hire an experienced GM? Either way works, as long as you, the owner, are focused on doing the right things, and making sure that your manager is doing things right, that is, those things that make a restaurant profitable. State the key positions of your management team. Give a brief description of the type of person you plan to hire in each and why he or she is best suited for that position. See Section III: The Nitty Gritty, Management.

Operational Systems: Define your operational systems, the navigational instruments and rudder of your great ship. They set the course, steering the ship on a straight and smooth course. How will you ensure training, consistent ongoing operations, and effective controls? This should be summarized in your Business Plan. See Section III: The Nitty Gritty, Operational Systems.

Financial Requirements: Show your financial requirements in four primary areas:

1. Construction build-out cost per square Foot
2. FF&E (furniture, fixtures & equipment), including the décor package—pictures/paintings, etc.
3. Professional fees: legal, accounting, architectural, licenses, permits, and miscellaneous fees
4. Working capital: enough for opening inventories, pre-opening expenses such as training, and staying power while the business revs up

See Section III: The Nitty Gritty, Financial Requirement.

Interior Floor Plan and Elevation Renderings: In this section of your business plan, you will need to provide a floor plan and elevation rendering of your restaurant. A picture is worth a thousand words, as the saying goes, which is why these renderings are crucial. See Section III: The Nitty Gritty, Interior Floor Plan and Elevation Renderings.

Sales, Profit & Loss Projections: This section should show, in spreadsheet format, sales projections, which are critical to establishing a budget. The sum of rent, food costs, and labor costs subtracted from sales will determine the majority of your bottom line. See Section III: The Nitty Gritty, Sales, Profit & Loss Projections.

Section III:
The Nitty Gritty

The Nitty Gritty is not part of your business plan. It would make the business plan cumbersome, bogged down with detail that is of no interest to a prospective investor or lender. Remember, a business plan has dual purposes: It can be used to acquire capital; but it is also a road map to where you are going and how you expect to get there. Therefore, in order for you to successfully open your restaurant, it is essential for you to learn and understand the Nitty Gritty of your business plan in as much detail as possible.

THE COMPANY STRUCTURE

Here, you must consult a lawyer and certified public account (CPA) to establish the best business entity for you. Unless you already have an established business with substantial assets that satisfy the requirements for your lease and bank loan, you will almost always be required to personally sign and guarantee the lease and any loans. Sub S Corps, or Limited Liability Corps (LLC), are usually the best way to go for a small business. A full corporation entity will give you no personal protection, if you're personally guaranteeing contracts, and you'll wind up paying corporate taxes, in addition to personal taxes on profits distributed. Sub S Corporations and LLCs allow you to pay personal taxes only on distributions of company profits.

Partnerships can be very good, or very bad. Profits can be distributed equally in a partnership, or not. However, it is better to have one person steering the ship. Keep personal egos out of the equation.

Make your decision on a partner's role in the company based on their background, experience, abilities, and business acumen. Choose one decision maker, with the other partners acting in support roles. Based upon each partner's demonstrated expertise, try to place partners in those positions that will complement the whole, rather than breed conflict about who is responsible for what.

Ideally, the partner chosen to run the restaurant should be the *general partner* in a Limited Liability partnership. The advantage to this arrangement is that the general partner has complete authority on all operational decisions. This can be vital to a smooth running and profitable operation, free of conflicts caused by differing operational opinions from outside investors. The trade off on this is that the general partner assumes all liability and the limited partners have no liability other than their initial investment.

Establishing your company, your business entity, is one of the first elements from your business plan for you to address. All permits, licensing, and vendor contracts will originate with your business entity.

RESTAURANT SERVICE CATEGORIES

Are you going to have table service with a wait and bus staff in the dining room and a chef in the kitchen, or the limited staff of a fast-food or fast-casual service food outlet? This is not only an important factor in making your three-legged stool concept work, but determines your labor costs, which are pegged to the experience and expertise of your staff.

The basic restaurant service categories are as follows: sit-down table service; fast-food; fast-casual. Additionally, there are sub-categories offered by many restaurants, especially in larger cities, like catering and delivery service. Either can stand separately or be an integrated part of your restaurant.

The restaurant category is defined by its service system, its décor, menu choices, and menu prices.

The first category, sit-down table service, is a more traditional restaurant concept and is basically the one most familiar in the Western world. Most European countries still prefer this method of dining and service. It can be a low price, simple Mom & Pop diner/café, or a one-dimensional coffee shop; or it can be a high price, gourmet white-tablecloth, fine dining restaurant. What will distinguish it from others in this category are its superb menu choices, higher menu prices, and excellent service.

Because it is a destination in itself, the sit-down, fine dining restaurant is not as dependent on name recognition as the fast-food or fast-casual restaurant. Convenience and low prices are the key attractions of a McDonald's or Burger King, fulfilling the needs of the impulse, grab a quick-bite-to-eat customer.

There are relatively few sit-down, fine-dining restaurants that are franchises, compared to fast-food or fast-casual restaurants. A fine-dining establishment takes a great deal more management experience and expertise to operate, while franchises are designed for simplicity—not lending themselves to the complexities of operating a fine-dining restaurant.

Customer expectations are a significant part of the dining experience. It's only natural to expect more at a restaurant known for its exquisite food and service, where you are paying more than a fast-food or fast-casual restaurant. Expectations are normally a bit higher at a fast-casual than a fast-food restaurant; and expectations are highest of all at a fine-dining restaurant. The typical frequent diner at a fine-dining restaurant is generally affluent and will demand the best in food, service, and atmosphere; anything less won't cut it.

The second category, fast-food, is a by-product of the American lifestyle. It evolved over a relatively short time because it met the needs of the go-go generation, the expanding middle class, with less time on their hands because of the competitive economy. The fast-food category can best be described as simply prepared, inexpensive food, served (you guessed it) fast. Because of the ease of preparation, minimal expertise and labor are required, and menu prices are at the low end of the restaurant spectrum.

Most successful fast food restaurants are franchises. Name recognition is important for these outlets because they depend on impulse driven customers. Moreover, a franchisee of a national chain will benefit from the franchisors' huge outlays of advertising dollars on television and other media (who doesn't remember a McDonald's jingle?). In addition to name recognition, fast food franchises are normally successful because they are the simplest to operate and require the least amount of experience by the owner/operator.

Though price driven, the fast food customer is no less quality-conscious than someone who is willing to pay more. In addition to expecting good value for the price, he or she expects fast service.

Convenience, budget, and a limited time schedule drive these customers to a fast-food outlet.

The third category, fast-casual, is the latest entry in restaurant concepts. It evolved from a combination of the best features of table service and fast food. Fast-casual delivers the speedy service of fast-food, but the ambiance and menu items are generally of a higher quality. Though marginally more expensive than fast-food, fast-casual fare costs far less than what you'd expect to pay at a sit-down table service restaurant. Fast-casual is the fastest growing segment of the restaurant industry today. Like other restaurant concepts, its success has everything to do with timing. The growing American middle class expects more quality and more creativity in its food today, but our fast lifestyle hasn't changed. Fast-casual fits this demand to a T.

Fast-casual appeals to many segments of our society today. A typical example would be a young family with children at home. The father and mother both work and either one, or both, prepares dinner for the family at night. Occasionally, mom or dad will stop at a grocery deli or restaurant and bring home a prepared meal. Assume that one or two nights a week both parents are tired and look forward to a relaxing dinner out with the family. The kids are too young to enjoy two hours at a high-end table service restaurant and their parents wouldn't want to spend the money anyway. Yet, they are looking forward to a dining experience better than a burger and fries, something with a better atmosphere and menu selection but with moderate pricing and the fast service that fast-food chains offer. Fast-casual restaurants fit these couples' needs perfectly—they can enjoy a good dinner and can get in and out quickly and home in time for Letterman.

Note that both fast-casual and fast-food appeal to a breakfast and lunch market for the same reasons: speed of service, menu selections, atmosphere, and price. But fast-casual transcends fast-food because it better satisfies the high expectations for food, service, and atmosphere, yet is value-conscious and delivers the same convenience of a fast-food chain.

Each of these restaurant categories can be successful if located properly. However, a location that may work for one may not work for another. For example, fast-food outlets typically flourish in middle-class and blue collar neighborhoods. A high-end, expensive, white tablecloth concept will not work in that same neighborhood but will in a more affluent demographic area. Fast-casual can work in both but, typically, fast-casual depends on a strong lunch business. A high density of daytime employment is needed to make a fast-casual res-

taurant thrive. An ideal location is one with white collar office buildings in an industrial park that are one to three miles away and easily
driven to. If your restaurant is close to a residential area with a high
density of mid- to high-level income families, your dinner trade will
also flourish.

There are three major factors to consider when choosing your restaurant category and concept:

1. Is there a proven and established market for your concept in your
   chosen area? Avoid trying to create a new consumer market for
   your concept; concentrate instead on coming up with a better
   application of the concept to fit an already established market.

2. Based on financial projections, can you expect your restaurant to
   produce gross annual sales of one to two times your initial investment? You will need those types of sales to make your return on
   investment worthwhile and prudent. For example, if your restaurant is going to cost $700,000 to open, and your sales projections
   indicate annual sales of $300,000, with a net profit of 15%, you
   can see that it is a bad investment.

3. Unless you can net 15% to 20% profit, consider investing your
   money elsewhere. In order to make a 15% to 20% profit, you will
   need to make Points1 & 2 a reality; and you will also need to
   exercise additional cost controls. Rent, for instance, should not
   exceed 10% of your gross sales. An 8% rent factor is good, and
   6% or lower is terrific. Your combined food and beverage costs
   should not exceed 30%, and your labor costs should be in the low
   to mid 20% level.

In creating the concept for your dream restaurant, be sure to focus
on how it corresponds to the category you have in mind. Follow the
three-legged milking stool idea: food, atmosphere, service. Be sure
the three legs work together, and you'll be way ahead of the game.
Think of any successful restaurant or chain, like Starbucks. Notice
how the three separate elements combine seamlessly to make the
whole. What on the surface appears to be just another coffee shop is,
in reality, far more. Starbucks' management team has created the "in
place to be," a modern-day meeting place for business associates and
friends who bring their laptops and newspapers and enjoy the ambiance and camaraderie. Starbucks' formula for success resides in the
quality of its imaginative coffee drinks, relaxing atmosphere of warm
colors and casual seating, and the careful selection and training of its

staff. The three basic ingredients I stress throughout this book—atmosphere, product quality, and service-oriented employees—are all at work there. All three work together as a whole to form the company's astonishing success.

You can be creative with your concept by simply using variations of other successful concepts, as long as you follow the three-legged rule. I honestly don't believe I have ever had a purely original idea. I simply focused on a well known and successful theme, and then I took a little here and a little there from what I considered the best of the best, and voila: I created an *original*.

Think about this; it's not rocket science. Once the concept of the original wheel was conceived, others who followed proceeded to improvise and create *original* variations of the wheel that are in use today everywhere you look: wheels for producing retail products, wheels and tires for all manner of transportation, wheels for hydraulic power and energy, wheels for toys and games. Most athletic games revolve around some type of ball, the vast majority of which are round. The list of *original* ideas derived from the original wheel idea is almost infinite. So do not worry too much about being original. Just be *creatively* original.

Being truly creative is thinking outside the box. It's a fact that almost every significant breakthrough in the field of science is first a break with tradition. Think of the evolution of the restaurant business in the US It began with the European table service style of restaurant, evolved into fast-food in the US, and now into fast-casual. Each category and concept in the restaurant business has its roots in the past, but true genius is moving your idea into the future. Keep in mind that the restaurant industry is constantly evolving and changing with the needs of the consumer. What works today may not work ten years from now. What works ten years from now...you get the picture.

There's a classic story known to most successful restaurateurs. It involves the restaurant owner standing in the middle of his restaurant's empty dining room. He is deeply frustrated, agonizing over the fact that ten years ago he had a line out the door every night but, today, his clientele has largely vanished. "Today I have no business and I am doing the same things now that I did ten years ago," he moans to himself. If only he understood the irony. He just answered his own question: he failed to change with the times and is still doing the same things he did ten years ago, without taking note of the changes within his market.

I used the example of Starbucks as a new and creative idea that evolved from an old coffeehouse concept. Consider how McDonalds has changed over the years, and continues to do so. You would not recognize the original McDonalds of yesteryear when you walk into any of the new McDonalds outlets today. Chalk it up to a smart, ahead-of-the-curve management team at headquarters in Illinois.

SERVICE

Whatever your chosen concept, good customer service should always be an integral part of it. Good service is far more than just efficient service. Service begins with an attitude of "I am here to be of service to you," not "I am doing you a favor." Unfortunately, an occasional, unpleasant attitude from servers is something we have all experienced at one time or another, and it invariably left a bad taste in our mouths.

Certain aspects of service will differ depending on the category of restaurant, whether one dispensing white tablecloth service, or the more casual environment of fast-food or fast-casual. However, there is one constant that will transcend all restaurant categories: an employee's attitude toward the customer. Most consumers will forgive an honest mistake. However, they will not forgive rude or indifferent service. A typical consumer will interpret an indifferent attitude not only as bad service but as a personal and direct insult.

The employment interview is an indispensable tool in making sure you are selecting the right people with the right attitude. Hiring the first person you interview only perpetuates your problem. Next week, you will be hiring someone else to replace that person. Know exactly what type of person you are looking for, not just the work experience that qualifies them for the job, but the personal attitude toward life in general, and people in particular.

The restaurant business is a people business. Even if a prospective employee's position does not entail dealing with the public, he or she must still mix well with fellow workers and consider themselves members of a team. You can train most anyone in the mechanics of a job. What is more difficult to overcome is the person with poor people skills and a negative attitude. Trying to motivate a person who habitually sees the glass as half empty rather than half full is both frustrating and a waste of your time and energy.

Develop your own employee interview questionnaire that you feel will best identify the type of employee you want. I used such a questionnaire years ago while working as a consultant. One of the questions on the list was: "What would you say to a customer who tells you that your food and service are terrible?" One client thought that the question was rather silly, because common sense dictates that you try and do everything possible to make the customer happy. I suggested to the client that she interview the next interviewee, a well-groomed young lady who, on the surface, appeared to be a great asset to the wait staff. The client asked her the same question and received this answer: "I would tell them then, if they felt that way, they should leave and not bother coming back." Interesting, isn't it, how deceiving looks can be?

It's obvious that good service begins by making the right choice in the selection of employees. The goals of hiring can be condensed to two:

- Hire only those people who will project the image that you have defined for your restaurant, both in appearance and attitude.
- Hire and train people you feel will remain committed to your operation, thus reducing employee turnover and effecting a smoother, more profitable operation.

Being aware of the most common reasons why employees leave a job is invaluable in hiring the right people and retaining them as employees. Reducing employee turnover is a key goal of a good manager. Here are some common reasons expressed by employees for leaving a job:

- The company doesn't care.
- A lack of rules or lack of consistent application of rules that exist.
- The company doesn't keep its promises.
- Pay is not very good.
- Manager gave me the wrong impressions of the job before I was hired.
- Lack of training.
- Little recognition of accomplishment ("Nobody ever thanks me!").
- Low morale within the organization.
- Unfair scheduling of hours.
- Lack of awareness of department or company goals.

The rules of customer service can be taught through a good training program and reinforced by the vigilance of management (low-key, always!). However, *attitude* is an intangible that is far more difficult to pin down. Rather than being taught, the right attitude must be spontaneously demonstrated.

If I could pick one example from the *Customer Service Handbook* that best demonstrates why I've been successful in this business, it would be the following: I was managing the floor one evening at the first Hungry Farmer shortly after it opened. A new staff member came to me with a question: A customer requested buttermilk, even though buttermilk was not on the menu. Did we have any? I told the waiter to tell the customer that we did not, but if he would give us ten minutes, he'd have all the buttermilk he could drink. I then jumped in my car, raced to a nearby supermarket, and bought a quart of buttermilk. Needless to say, we had a customer who was extremely satisfied (nearly stunned!) by our service. What is the ultimate lesson here? Go the extra mile, and you'll have a customer for life.

It was a spontaneous action on my part but did more to show my employees what good service was than anything in our training manual. Employees will always look to the manager for leadership by example. It beats mere words every time.

Then there are those missed opportunities. Here's one, told to me by a friend who witnessed an exchange in a national fast-casual chain restaurant. My friend was in line, ready to order, behind a young couple. The young man had given the cashier a credit card that was declined. The cashier then called the manager for direction. The manager began by telling the young couple that when a credit card was declined, it usually meant the card was stolen. The young man protested that it was not stolen. Unfortunately, he had no other form of payment. My friend intervened by paying for the young couple's meal. The missed opportunity? The manager should never have inferred that the card was stolen, but rather that it was "probably a mistake" and the meal was on him this time. Instead, he chose to embarrass the young couple, and most likely lost two customers for life.

Here are a few broad and encompassing tips on what constitutes outstanding service:

1. Outstanding service begins with the attitude of management. Management always sets the tone by caring for each customer, and going out of the way to make the customer's experience memorable. Management cannot set this example by sitting in the office during peak dining hours. As the symbol of quality food

and service, managers are a warm, welcoming presence for customers as they "talk the talk and walk the walk."

2. Outstanding service begins with hiring employees who have an attitude of "I am happy to be of service to you." The good service attitude is reinforced with positive reinforcement by management.

3. Outstanding service is maintained by repetitive training.

4. Outstanding service is making sure that the last customer of the evening receives the same service as the first.

5. Outstanding service begins with a cheerful and sincere greeting. "A greeting without a smile is like a kiss without a squeeze."

6. Outstanding service is making each customer feel like they are the most important person in your restaurant from the time they enter to the time they leave.

7. Outstanding service implies treating the restaurant as an extension of your home, where you pay special attention to details, like keeping the bathrooms spotless and always stocked with soap and towels.

8. Outstanding service is emptying overflowing trash containers, replacing lights that are burned out, and picking up trash in the parking lot.

9. Outstanding service is reporting for your shift on time and showing you care about your job.

10. Outstanding service is about telephone etiquette—answering the phone with a smile in your voice.

11. Outstanding service is about a heartfelt "thank you for letting us be of service to you."

12. Outstanding service is attentiveness to your customers' needs. A perceptive waiter or waitress can tell from across the room if a customer needs something by the customer's body language.

13. Outstanding service in a fast-food or fast-casual restaurant is often rendered by a cashier through a cheerful greeting and knowledge of the menu and the specials of the day.

14. Outstanding service is when you make a mistake and you apologize even before the customer knows of the mistake. When you anticipate a problem, you can diminish its impact to the customer with a sincere apology first. Customers know that stuff happens and can forgive mistakes when they know that you are aware and concerned about their satisfaction.

15. Finally, outstanding service is about going the extra mile and doing the unexpected. When a customer waits a few minutes longer for a table than quoted, the manager buys them a drink or dessert.

Nordstrom's department store is known for its exceptional service. There is a well-known story about a person who returned a tire to Nordstrom's because he was dissatisfied, for one reason or another. As the story goes, Nordstrom's accepted the tire with full credit, despite something rather unusual for most businesses: Nordstrom's does not sell tires.

In one of my restaurants, we once served a table of four where one person at the table bitterly complained that his steak was inedible. I could have told the customer that we had sold two hundred steaks that evening without a complaint. Or, I could have ordered him another steak or just have told him that there would be no charge for his meal with an apology. What I did was to go beyond the expected and comped it; that is, I picked up the tab for the entire table of four diners. What could have been a negative experience turned into an amazing evening for those four customers, one they will never forget. How many people do you suppose they told of that unusual gesture of "going beyond the expected"?

At the Hungry Dutchman in Denver, a waiter decided to put a little extra showmanship in his service. We served coffee from silver coffee pots. The innovative waiter pinched the end of the spout on the coffee pot so that the coffee would pour in a thin stream. By doing this, he was able to hold the coffee cup in a low position in one hand and pour from the coffee pot in a high position in the other hand. Customers loved it. Soon all the wait staff were doing the same *high pour* and developing new and even more innovative ways of serving coffee, for example, pouring coffee over their shoulder behind their back, or placing the coffee cup on their shoe top while balancing on one leg and pouring the coffee, and other conversation stoppers. I would be remiss if I didn't tell you I experienced some anxious moments watching these antics, but the customers loved it and the staff was motivated by it.

All is not sugar and spice in this business, however. Here's an embarrassing mistake I made in the early stages of my career at the North Woods Inn. It was a Saturday night and, as usual, we were running an hour wait for a table. Our system for parties without advance reservations was a form with a column for the customers' names, the wait-time quoted, and the time that they arrived. One lady, who had no reservation and to whom I had initially quoted an hour wait, came up fifteen minutes after she had arrived and said that she had been waiting over an hour. I politely showed her the reservation sheet, pointing out the time quoted and the time that she had arrived. It was obvious that this lady had been enjoying a cocktail or two. She proceeded to come back every ten minutes and I would patiently repeat the same explanation. Finally, out of exasperation, I suggested that perhaps she had indulged in one cocktail too many, and perhaps she wasn't completely accurate in remembering the time she had arrived. BIG MISTAKE! Within minutes, a giant of a young man approached me with mayhem in his manner and a challenge in his voice. "Did you call my mother a drunk?" he asked. Needless to say, I apologized profusely, and within minutes they had a table and their dinner was on me.

Most training is done on the job and is focused on the mechanics of the job. However, employee meetings can be used for instilling and maintaining the attitude of service. Role playing can emphasis good or bad service with explicit examples of good or bad service.

Employee meetings can be an effective place to offer employees important reminders about service. Emphasize these issues:

- How valuable our customer really is and what a normal customer's service expectations may be.
- The customer is the most important person to our business.
- The customer is not dependent on the restaurant but the restaurant and its employees are dependent on the customer.
- Our number one objective is to make our customers happy.
- A satisfied customer is a positive advertisement for the restaurant and an unhappy customer the opposite.
- A successful restaurant needs to create a large core of repeat customers and the most effective way to do that is with exceptional food and service.
- Customers have many restaurant choices, so we have to give them a better reason to comeback than our competitors do.

Outstanding service must be constantly reinforced to your staff. A short pre-shift meeting with the serving staff can be vital to putting them in the right mind set of a *service* attitude. A short pre-shift meeting with the kitchen staff will reinforce the importance of quality preparation, plate presentation, and speed. Outstanding service reminder signs in employee areas can reinforce the habit of outstanding service.

Most restaurant management will emphasize suggestive selling to their staff as a way of increasing their check average, tip income, and restaurant sales. While suggestive selling can increase sales in the short term, it can have an adverse effect on repeat business. It is important that the server be familiar with the menu and make positive suggestions to help a customer's menu selection. However, if the restaurant guest perceives that the server is just trying to build the check and not genuinely concerned for their satisfaction by trying to be helpful, they will be offended and not likely to come back.

The last point that I want to make on service is always strive for the WOW factor. When you ask a customer how was their meal and service, and you do not hear a WOW factor in their reply, than you have work to do.

Motivation: Service begins and is maintained through positive motivation. Motivation then transcends into inspiration.

The policies and operational systems of restaurant management are critically important. However, they are only parts of a smooth running vehicle that will take you on your journey to success. The essential element to your vehicle is motivated employees. The good manager understands this intrinsically and, through his or her leadership, constantly provides and maintains the right balance of motivation that inspires the restaurant's staff.

The best rule of thumb for motivating your employees is to reinforce the positive when you see them performing at a high level of excellence, and reward them for it. Here's a book I heartily recommend that you read. Called *The One Minute Manager*, it's a small book with a big message about a management style that is so simple and so essentially human.

Here's a quick illustration from my own experience about what the book is about. I had a consulting client several years ago, a gentleman living on the east coast, who consulted with me about problems he was having with his restaurant. His location was excellent, one which fit his customer demographics and restaurant concept to a T. He should have been very successful. However, he had a major problem: extremely difficult labor issues. Every day was an adventure in how many of the scheduled staff would show up. His restaurant was a revolving door. If an employee lasted a month, they were considered old-timers.

Immediately clear to me was that the owner was not very personable, nor was he supportive or reassuring towards his employees. I tried to be diplomatic in implying that this might be at the heart of his labor problems. One day, I called to see how business was progressing. He informed me that he was incredulous about an incident with an employee that had just taken place. The employee was making a sandwich for a customer while the customer stood at the counter and watched. A piece of meat fell off the unfinished sandwich onto the cutting board. The employee picked it up and replaced it on the sandwich. The owner, feeling this was improper procedure, grabbed the sandwich and threw it in the trash. He then proceeded to remake a new sandwich for the customer himself. The employee calmly took off his apron and walked out the door. The owner could not understand how the employee could be so unprofessional and irresponsible. I tried to explain to him than even if the employee had not made the sandwich exactly to procedure, that there were better ways to handle it than the way he had.

I tried explaining the management concept of "reinforcing positive behavior with positive feedback, as opposed to negative feedback." A better alternative would have been to let the employee finish making the sandwich. Then, in the privacy of the manager's office, explain the mistake to him. As it was, the employee walked out because he was humiliated in front of his peers and the customer.

I followed up this conversation with a mailed copy of *The One Minute Manager.* When I later called to see what he thought of the book, his response was, "Why should I worry about patting them on the back when I am paying them good money to do the job?"

Our consulting client went broke and was out of business within a year. He sold the business to an experienced restaurant operator who understood how to motivate his employees. Within a very short time, the new owner had a happy and loyal staff and a thriving and profitable business.

Motivating employees requires time and a sincere effort on your part. It is something that comes from the heart and is demonstrated by having pride in your people and your restaurant. Additionally, it is maintaining a consistent attitude of not only wanting to be the best, but by working with your staff to make them the best. It is a sincere attitude of caring about your fellow man and woman. You cannot manipulate others for very long, if at all. They will soon see that your motives are not about them, but about your own selfish needs.

Read *The One Minute Manager.* If it does not resonate with you, then I suggest that you not consider the restaurant business.

Restaurant employees, for the most part, are not your normal, career-oriented people. Some are students who need a little extra beer money; some are professional people who were laid off from their jobs and are temporarily "floating," and some are housewives who have the time, but could use a little extra financial help now that the kids are in school. You'll even find a sprinkling of senior citizens, who, bored and craving something to do with their lives, turn to restaurant work. Restaurant help comes in all types, all ages, and all with their own reasons to give the business a try.

And that's what a smart manager must understand about his potential employees: that a large percentage of a restaurant staff usually lack a specific career direction in life and, are thus not terribly motivated to begin with. They're not homeless or downtrodden; however, many feel that the world takes more than it gives. They are not accustomed to a boss who cares more about them than the boss's own personal interests. Certainly not a boss who goes out of his way to treat them with respect and dignity! To illustrate: cleaning the outside trash area is an unpopular job, but one that must be attended to. Normally, this job is part of the dishwasher job description. As a manager, I could simply tell the dishwasher to clean the garbage area. He knows that's his job, so why bother to add anything more than "just do it"? However, the more positive approach is to recognize the dishwasher's professionalism—take him aside and remind him of how important cleanliness is to all areas of the restaurant, both inside and outside. I would also thank him in advance for doing a job that you both know is as much fun as following a parade of elephants with a pooper scooper.

Your overall attitude toward your employees will always be the greatest motivator, hands down. However, you'll find it quite helpful to know what specifically motivates each of your employees, and treat them accordingly. Most employees are motivated by increased pay. Some are motivated by increased status and responsibility, and some are motivated by other rewards. Keep in mind, though, that you cannot motivate an employee with just a pay increase or increased status, or any other means without a positive, personal expression of appreciation of a job well done. It has been my experience, proven many times over, that all employees are motivated by a sincere attitude of caring for them as a person, and not just someone to be used to accomplish company objectives.

For those employees motivated by increased pay, the solution is simple. Define very clearly what you consider the kind of work deserving of a raise—arriving to work on time, staying on task, helping customers and co-workers, etc.—and tell them that if they exceed your expectations, they have earned the right to a raise in pay. Arrange a time in the future when you will evaluate how he or she is doing and, at that time, grant a raise or explain exactly why a raise is not in order. If you do offer a raise in pay, be sure and remind your employee that an increase in responsibility comes with the increase in pay.

For employees who are interested in moving up the chain of command and are motivated by increased status and responsibility, the solution is similar to those motivated by money. Define clearly what you expect. Tell them that if they master those duties and responsibilities you expect of them and prove they can lead by example, you will delegate even more responsibility to them. If they take a professional attitude in their job, exceeding your expectations, consider offering them a title, such as Lead Trainer, Head Cashier, Shift Leader, and the like. Allowing them to run a shift during the slow days of the week, and giving them some—albeit small—authority over other employees, will go a long way in creating pride in their work and your restaurant. Remember, though, delegating more tasks and giving employees more authority does not remove the responsibility from management. Management must closely monitor how the employee handles his or her increased responsibility and status.

For employees who are motivated by other rewards, management must often get creative. Some employees, especially younger ones, are disinterested in getting a raise or promotion, and simply want to *get stuff,* or be rewarded in different ways. There is no set way to motivate these kinds of employees, but coming up with different techniques can be fun as well as challenging. Some motivational tools work wonders, like giving away concert tickets; or granting a day of no cleaning duties for employees that perform exceptionally well in cleaning during the week or month. Additionally, offering a free day, where an employee can pick any day of the month to have a paid day off, can be a strong motivator for employees who clock in on time every day they are scheduled to work. (This really works well for high-school students who do a good job, but are often unreliable.)

The effective leader understands and accepts the following time-tested premise: "There are no rewards and there is no punishment; there are only the consequences of my actions." A truly good leader takes responsibility for those consequences of his or her actions. I had a sign in my office for years that sums up this idea. It was a caricature of the president of a company, sitting behind his desk and exclaiming angrily that he was "surrounded by nothing but idiots!" The caption under the picture said it all: "Meet the head idiot." No cop outs. No excuses. You're the one who hires and trains your staff. You're the one who leads and motivates your staff by example.

I remember once pulling up in front of a restaurant to have dinner. The best parking spot in the lot was right next to the front door, with *Owner Parking* in big letters on the concrete block that fronted the parking space. I didn't bother to go in because I knew what the experience would be like.

I am paraphrasing this quote, but it goes something like this: "Begin with a thought that leads to an action which becomes a habit which results in your destiny." Effective motivation begins and ends with leadership that focuses on others, and not on self. If my thought process is focused on me, my actions will be self-centered in nature, reinforced by habit, and will continually reflect this. Any attempt at motivation will be considered to be manipulative and self-serving by your staff. What kind of message do you think that owner, with the prime parking space identified as his alone, was giving to his employees?

I once had signs made that I hoped conveyed the right message to my managers, and placed them in the offices of all my restaurants. The sign was an inverted pyramid. At the top of the pyramid was the customer; next came the staff; then the manager; and, at the bottom, the president of the company. If the manager's first goal is to serve the needs of the staff, it will result in better serving the needs of the customer.

Athletic teams are mostly successful because they have the right leadership. The leaders, from coaches to captains, know that the team's success comes from good chemistry among every member of the organization and team. Each member of the team must work toward a common goal—victory—which is more easily achieved when everyone adopts the attitude of "one for all and all for one." No one team member is more important than any other; each is just a part of the whole. They win together, they lose together, and they strive to improve together. Lou Holtz, the legendary football coach who produced championship teams at three different universities, said it best: "A great team can beat great athletes." This is a principle definitely worth remembering when you open your first restaurant.

Motivating employees is achieved best by letting them work toward a goal that offers them personal gratification and success. You cannot motivate an employee for a set period of time to reach a short-term goal; try and you become more of a cheerleader than a leader. Half-time speeches alone achieve short term results.

Management's job in keeping employees self-motivated is to provide continual, follow-up training. This gives them the incentive to improve their skills and increase their knowledge base. To this end, managers become teachers or coaches, constantly sharing their knowledge and experience for the benefit of their employees...which leads to the success of your restaurant.

I once had an employee who was mentally challenged. We worked with him on learning the skills of properly running the dishwashing machine. Because we took the time in providing encouragement and support from the entire staff, he became the best dishwasher in the business, and one of the finest employees I ever had the privilege to work with. He worked in the same position, as head dishwasher, at one of my restaurants for over twelve years.

When I speak of sincerely caring about the employees as part of effective leadership, it reminds me of one of my favorite allegories: A man dreams that he is in a room with two doors. Neither door is marked, yet he intuitively knows that behind one door is heaven and behind the other door is hell. He opens the first door and finds a long table with an abundance of exquisite, gourmet food. Surrounding the table are hundreds of people who are emaciated from starvation and screaming in frustration. They all have long spoons in their hands and are frantically digging into the food with the spoons. The problem is that the spoons are so long that they cannot get the food into their mouths. He slams the door shut and says to himself, *This must surely be hell.* Upon opening the second door, he finds a similar table with the same abundance of wonderful cuisine. However, the hundreds of people surrounding this particular table are happy and well fed. They all have long spoons, too, but the difference is that they are feeding one another, rather than trying to feed themselves.

There is overwhelming evidence that the higher the level of self-esteem, the more likely one will treat others with respect, kindness, and generosity. It has been my experience that there is a reverse effect to this as well. The more one treats others with respect, kindness, and generosity, the more self-esteem one acquires.

Allow me one more personal example of unintended but subtle employee motivation, and how powerful it can be. A few years back, my wife and I received an invitation to attend a renewal of marital vows ceremony. The invitation was from a waitress who had formerly worked for me. She and her husband were celebrating fifty years of marriage. Frankly, I was surprised at the invitation and curious why, after over thirty years, I would be invited to such a personal and special event.

The ceremony took place in the back yard of their modest home under an arbor of flowers. Both bride and groom were dressed in their original wedding attire. (Their daughters had done a great deal of letting out and sewing to show their parents at their best.) I was immediately struck by the fact that the vast majority of people there were family: their children, grandchildren, and other family members. There were only a few close family friends there besides my wife and me. We could not help but wonder—why had we been invited to such an intimate, personal ceremony?

After the ceremony and during the reception, the bride, Pauline, approached me and asked if I was wondering why I had been invited. I had to admit that, yes, I had been surprised and was quite curious. She then reminded me of an incident from the long-forgotten past. Pauline was one of my original staff members at the first Hungry Farmer and we had worked together for several years. She told me of a time she had approached me and asked for a company loan to have some extensive dental work done. I had told her that it was against company policy to make loans to employees. However, I let her know that company policy had nothing to do with me giving her a personal loan. Pauline then told me she had never forgotten my generosity and how much it had meant to her. That long-ago gesture was not really one of generosity; it was simply helping a friend in need.

Most clear thinking people enjoy looking good, perhaps even to the point of showing off a little. In order to look good, employees will do their work the way they think it should be done. However, that is not always the correct way. By showing the employee a better way (to look good), they are motivated and inspired. Additionally, when they know that they are doing their job well and are verbally rewarded for a job well done, they become addicted to that good feeling of approval.

When this happens to one or two employees, it sets a mood that is infectious. No one wants to be different from the group. Most want to fit in and be accepted, so they will follow the norm in their workplace environment.

There can be a fine line between effective management and motivation. Clearly, it is the responsibility of management to see that certain procedures and policies are followed by their employees. As the boss, the manager can rigidly enforce them. An enlightened manager empowers their employees to make the right decisions through proper training and then takes the risk of giving them the freedom to do their job without micromanaging them. If a manager feels that they must micromanage, then they have not hired the right people or trained them sufficiently.

Trying to blatantly control the behavior of another human being is demeaning to that person. Properly preparing employees to do their job well is really all management can do. After that, trying to control behavior is futile. That being said, there will be employees who must be released if they do not respond to management's training and positive reinforcement.

Employee empowerment allows everyone to relax and enjoy their jobs. Conversely, a transparently controlled environment can be perceived by customers and make them uncomfortable.

MENU

In designing your menu, always begin with what you personally feel would be the right menu for your concept. Don't focus only on what is practical and functional. By focusing only on the practical aspects of a menu, you will lose inspiration and creativity.

Only after you have settled on what you think are the most appealing items for your menu is it time to consider their practicality. Cost of product is a main consideration. For example, if your concept is fast-casual, then your price point will probably be in the $8.00 to $14.00 range. But since the wholesale cost of lobster or a prime cut of New York steak takes you out of the fast-casual ballpark, they would not be compatible with the pricing of your menu.

Your pricing must reflect your décor and service. A high-end gourmet menu would be completely out of place in a fast food outlet, with its simple décor and speedy service.

Another consideration is the skill level of your employees. If you plan on opening a fast-food or fast-casual restaurant, you need to hire kitchen personnel whose skills are commensurate with a pay scale driven by your menu price points. Conversely, a gourmet, table-side service restaurant, with higher menu price points, requires a higher level of employee skills and experience, and obviously a more appropriate pay scale.

The equipment needed for certain menu items is an important factor. For example, do you need a grill, or a deep fat fryer? If so, then you will need to factor in the cost of a grease trap and a vented hood with fire suppression equipment. This can easily add $25,000 to $50,000 to your equipment package.

The tools and equipment for a restaurant may differ from those of a construction company, but both are equally critical to getting the job done correctly. In the restaurant industry, there are professionals who specialize in efficient kitchen design and can source the equipment you need to fit the demands of your menu. It is extremely important to select this person carefully. Make sure they have the experience and a proven history of positive results. A good consultant can tell you exactly what equipment is best-suited for your menu and show you a kitchen design that will maximize kitchen efficiency and minimize kitchen labor cost.

Inventory requirements are another essential factor. In designing a menu, how you determine its offerings is critical to controlling your food and labor costs. Consider the number of items on the menu: the more you offer the more labor hours it takes to prep and serve each dish in a timely manner. An excess in inventory is money sitting on the shelf. And, the more menu items and ingredient inventories you have to account for, the more waste you are likely to incur. An important corollary of this—think how to wheel menu items together. This means using the same food products in as many different menu selections as possible.

In my experience, I have found that smaller is better. What many neophytes in this business fail to realize when designing a menu is that more menu choices is not necessarily better. In fact, the more choices offered, the more they will cannibalize one another. An effective way to add menu items while effectively controlling food costs is to offer daily specials. This way you can continue to offer a variety of selections that will keep your menu appealing. In preparing specials, be careful to prepare just enough, so that you will run out by the end of the day. This will help to control unnecessary waste.

You cannot create a menu that will be all things to all people, so focus on what you specialize in. Success is predicated on having the best, not the most. When I see a sign on a restaurant specializing in "American, Chinese, and or Italian and Mexican," my conclusion is that they are trying to do too much, and therefore will not do any of it well.

Depending on your concept and location, a mid-morning, afternoon, or late night snack menu can add revenue to otherwise non-productive times.

A safe menu is one based on classic, traditional foods, to which you add your own unique twist. People have a comfort level with familiar foods. So, keep it simple, especially if you are new to the restaurant business. Quality of product and presentation will always be the foundation of your menu.

Next is speed and efficiency of service. The average customer in the US rates speed of service highly, and considers it part of the overall value received.

Smart menu choices are essential to a successful restaurant, but equally important is the presentation of your menu. The menu is what defines your restaurant. Customers browse through the menu and, with the help of a knowledgeable server, can make a well-informed selection.

The menu, however, is more than an information tool—it's also a valuable sales tool. Major considerations must be taken into account in menu design and production. Here are some time-tested rules to follow:

1. It must be functional and easy to use. A menu that is too big can be unwieldy for a customer to handle.

2. Your menu should convey the essence of your concept. Is it formal and sophisticated, or is it meant to be more fun and informal?

3. The menu should be integral to the customer's entire dining experience. The Hungry Farmer and the Hungry Dutchman menus shown in this book are good examples of conveying the fun, light-hearted atmosphere we wanted our customers to experience. The comic characters and humorous menu descriptions set the tone for a fun evening—a brief interlude from the worries of the day, a time to relax and enjoy fine food and drink.

4. Food and beverage descriptions are an important factor in your menu. More consumers today are interested in the details of what they are ordering. They don't need paragraphs of flowery words when ordering a steak, but its size and cut are essential; and some well-chosen, mouth-watering descriptions can seal the deal. Use descriptive adjectives for maximum appetite appeal. The more

creative you are, the more you enhance your menu offerings, making them more desirable. Paint a brief picture in your customers' minds with descriptive words like "steaming," "chilled," "garden fresh," "succulent," "juicy," etc.

5. Feature profitable and customer favorites with a picture of the item, highlighted by a brief description to stimulate the taste buds. Think of the clever merchandising that Starbucks uses on their menu boards—just the names of their coffee drinks suggest a tantalizing treat.

CUSTOMER PROFILE

Note: The target demographics given here are broad estimates based on my personal experiences. More specific and detailed information on restaurant category demographics can be found by contacting your local Restaurant Association, Chamber of Commerce, or the National Restaurant Association in Chicago, Illinois.

Your customer profile should fit your chosen restaurant category. Generally, the following customer profiles fit these corresponding categories: Fast-food is generally targeted to low- to mid-income level consumers. Depending on the geographic area of the country and its cost of living, targeted income demographics vary. Generally speaking, the fast-food target profile is a customer whose household income is lower than $50,000 per year.

In addition to the income demographic, the fast-food category also encompasses a wide age demographic. Both grade school and college-age customers fall into this category and are an excellent target market.

There are exceptions to predetermined market areas. For example, a fast-food restaurant can be successful in a high density white collar office environment as well as a blue collar industrial area. The problem here is that white collar, office park locations are generally high rent and weekend business can be slow to non-existent. Therefore, you would need to have a smaller space to afford the rent and your projections should show that you could be profitable on a five-day week schedule.

Fast-casual often overlaps with the demographics of fast-food. The ideal consumer target for this category is white collar, mid- to high-income level person, averaging $75,000 in household income with an average age in the range of 25 to 65. These customers have a busy lifestyle, so speed of service is paramount to them.

According to a *Restaurants & Institutions Magazine* article, dated September 1, 2007, "nearly 40% of mid- to high-income consumers say they visit fast-casual restaurants once a week or more, nearly twice the average of other categories." The same article goes on to say that "one third of these consumers are open to trying new restaurants in the fast-casual category, and many do." Moreover, "25% say they would eat at a particular restaurant more often if it were truly unique and different." Remember thinking outside the box? Here's your chance to come up with some creative ideas to make your restaurant unique.

Speed of service is most important to the fast-casual consumer. Décor, menu variety, and quality of food also rate highly. Typically, this target market is found in areas that include a mixture of high density office and residential communities of young families.

On the low-cost end of the sit-down table service category are small diners with inexpensive menus. Fast-food and fast-casual restaurants have hurt small diner business nationwide. Additionally, the small diner is generally equated with slower service than fast-casual or fast-food. All restaurants in the sit-down table service category require a wait staff and larger labor force than fast-food or fast-casual outlets.

Typically, the diner is found in small, rural area towns where the pace is slower and the demand for speed less important than in today's more hectic urban environment.

At the high end of sit-down table service is *fine dining*. The target market for this type of restaurant is limited. However, fine dining is highly desired by its consumer group. This customer base usually reflects an older, white collar demographic, with a household income in excess of $100,000.

This is the most expensive and challenging type of restaurant to open and operate. In order to make a fine dining restaurant a success, one must have a great deal more experience and knowledge than is needed in other restaurant categories. Labor costs are commensurate with the excellence this type of restaurant demands of its wait staff's skills. Also, the typical fine dining customer expects a certain amount of sophistication—up-scale décor is a given, along with superior professional service. The menu prices are higher, reflecting the greater cost of food and labor, but up-scale customers expect this: their demands and expectations are proportionate to the increased costs.

The high-end, sit-down table service restaurant consumer will react more to market economic conditions than fast-food or fast-casual consumers. In times of a slower economy, your typical high-end customer will eat out less frequently, or trade down to the fast-casual category.

COMPETITION

It is easier to get customers into your restaurant if they are already used to dining in the area. It's a lot easier when you don't have to educate the public about the location in a specific geographic area. Your primary goal is to persuade them to dine with you. There are many reasons why one area works for a certain category and not for another. Talk to owners of successful restaurants in different parts of town and they'll tell you why their restaurant's location was one of the keys to their success.

Research national chain restaurants in trade magazines, such as *Restaurant Institutions, Chain Leader,* or *Nation's Restaurant News,* three leading trade publications. They're a fund of valuable and profitable information on trends in the restaurant business. You can also do your own evaluation of sales by simply counting customers at specific restaurants, then multiplying that number by what you estimate the check averages to be. Remember, weekday customer counts will be less than weekends. Normally, Sunday and Monday will be the slowest days of the week, and Friday and Saturday the busiest.

Let me reiterate—one of the best ways of getting information about area competition is to talk directly to the ownership/management of the restaurants. There is a fraternal sentiment amongst most restaurant professionals. They are normally more than happy to share information with an aspiring restaurant entrepreneur. Additionally, they understand that the more good restaurant competition in their area, the better it is for their business.

MARKETING STRATEGY

I cannot stress enough the importance of a cohesive marketing strategy. Be sure it corresponds to the concept of your restaurant. Once you have grasped the profile of your target market, focus your marketing efforts on customers of that specific market within a one- to three-mile radius of your restaurant. If you truly understand your market and its potential customers, you don't need an expensive mass media advertising campaign to reach them.

Begin with the basic premise that all the advertising in the world will not work if you have not created and are not effectively applying the three-legged concept of food, atmosphere, and service. Getting the customer to your restaurant the first time is relatively easy; the trick is getting them to want to come back.

Mass media advertising is the easiest but most expensive way to attract customers and not necessarily the most effective. There are less expensive and more effective ways to reach the consumer. In an urban area, your customer base will live and work within a one to three mile area of your restaurant. The more urban your location, the more likely you'll have a higher density of potential customers within a short distance from your restaurant. In rural areas, the population base is more likely to be spread over a larger geographical area. Because there is less traffic, consumers are used to driving farther to fulfill their needs.

Mass media advertising in a larger population may not give you the best return on your investment. Advertising rates are based on circulation. Therefore, advertising dollars spent covering a large metropolitan area will cost more, even if your target market lives or works only one to three miles away.

Regardless of your marketing methods or outlay of dollars, your best advertising is your restaurant. And the best way to build your business is to get customers in the *first time*. Here's some advice you might be disposed to reject at first, but trust me—it works. I have always found that the best way to introduce a new restaurant to the public is by not charging your customers for their meals the first week you open. Obviously, you cannot advertise free food in the media— you would be overrun by freeloaders who have no intention of coming back. The trick is to reach a pre-selected target market, and treat each new customer like royalty.

Here are a few ideas of how to do that effectively:

1. Prior to the official opening of your restaurant, have flyers made up inviting specific businesses in your immediate market area for a free breakfast or lunch. On the flyer, state the day and time that the office is invited. Ask them to identify themselves by their business name. If you happen to get a few non-invited customers wandering in, that's all the better. Under no circumstances should

you turn anyone away. That would turn a positive into a negative for future business.

2. To create and maintain a dinner clientele, acquire selected zip code addresses in the immediate neighborhoods, and mail dinner invitations accordingly. The invitation should be simply stated— short and to the point: something like, "We'd like to invite you and your neighbors to visit our new restaurant and enjoy a delicious meal on us. The 'get acquainted' block party is next Monday night." State the times, and reinforce the dinner is on us, mentioning diplomatically (in small type) that alcohol is not included. Finish with a single line like, "We look forward to meeting you." Plan to do this for one full week. The money you spend on this type of marketing is far more personal and effective than media advertising. Make your entire menu free to these invited guests. Do not skimp by offering only selected inexpensive menu items. Your vendors will benefit from your restaurant getting off to a fast start as much as you will, so they will be happy to donate product. Sounds gutsy and expensive but, if done correctly, you'll discover this approach is far less expensive than a slow, drawn out process of building a customer base.

If you have properly pre-trained your employees and limited your invitees to a controllable number, you will give them a positive experience. This can also be a great training tool and highly motivational to your staff. Employees learn faster with live customer training and customers are certainly more tolerant and understanding of initial opening mistakes if their meal is free.

1. Try to personally meet and welcome as many of your new customers as possible. Each invited customer should be made to feel like a VIP; not just one of many in an impersonal mob scene. A successful restaurant entrepreneur knows that the restaurant business is a people business—highly personalized, one on one. Think of the occasion as a private party you're throwing for your personal friends. You'll be rewarded with repeat business, creating new customers with positive word-of-mouth that is the most effective advertising of all.

2. One-on-one community marketing, in which each customer is treated as a guest, takes a variety of forms that can work for you. Introduce yourself to the local church clergy. Let them know you would like to be on their list to participate in any special fund rais-

ing needs that may arise from time to time. For example, a special project for the church might be a two-week summer mission trip for high school church members. Your restaurant could give 10% of all proceeds on a special night, announced by the church to its members. You can even have high school members acting as hosts that evening, thanking people for supporting their cause.

3. Participating in local fund raisers shows you're a member of the community. Give senior and student discounts. Develop a database by asking customers to record their names and email addresses in your *Birthday Book*. On birthdays, send a happy birthday wish and a coupon for a free meal to the birthday celebrant. They will normally bring family and friends with them.

4. If you're located on a busy street with good visibility, select an employee with the biggest smile and place him or her in front of your restaurant with a sign advertising the special of the day. Drivers during busy traffic periods are often the same people who are aware of your new restaurant. By offering a different special each day of the week, chances are a driver will take a quick peek each day to see what the special is. Eventually, your drive-bys will know the day of their favorite special, and pull into the parking lot for lunch.

5. On a slow night (typically Monday) each month, try the following: Prepare a personalized letter for presentation to each table when customers have finished their meal. Keep it simple—along the lines of, "To thank you for your support and patronage, your dinner this evening is on the house. We look forward to seeing you again in the near future." In addition to spreading goodwill, you will be rewarded with a loyal clientele on your off night. You'll be amazed how quickly the word gets around about your generosity and how customers will begin flocking to your restaurant on Monday nights in the hopes that this could be the free Monday night. I would not include liquor purchases.

The Broker Restaurant, mentioned earlier, was located in an old bank in the financial district of downtown Denver. There was a large vault on the lower level of the building with the upper floors converted to a Dean Witter brokerage and various office suites.

Given the location in the heart of the downtown financial district, I figured we could do a terrific cocktail hour business with all the young executive men and women who worked in the area. I was right about the cocktail hour business in downtown Denver, but wrong about our location being able to get its share of it. The problem was visibility. Being in the basement of the building, the potential customer on the street could not easily look in. Those who did venture in to take a look at the new restaurant saw an attractive but empty cocktail lounge. They would take one look and then leave to where the action was; where people mingled, knew each other, or started up friendships. It's proven that the busier a bar, the more people flock to it for social hour.

If I could somehow get this popular period jump-started with a concept that was out of the box, I stood a good chance of establishing a respectable cocktail hour. Then the idea hit me: what better way to build a clientele than inviting each of the corporate offices, on different days of the week, for free hors d'oeuvres and drinks? I did this for two straight weeks, from four to seven P.M. The momentum grew, word-of-mouth quickly spread, and after two weeks of free hors d'oeuvres and drinks, we never looked back.

Cocktail hour at the Broker became an *in* thing in downtown Denver, and in order to handle the influx of business, we increased our staff to three bartenders and five cocktail waitresses.

With popularity comes the occasional wild happening: A well known professional golfer dropped by one evening, feeling no pain, and as the evening progressed, so did his idea of taking three of my cocktail waitresses with him to Las Vegas in his private jet. Unfortunately, the cocktail waitresses thought it would be fun, also. The manager called me for help. So the Broker manager, bookkeeper, and yours truly became the cocktail service staff: so much for employee loyalty. As a cocktail waiter, I must confess I did okay; I collected more in tips for a few hours serving martinis and Tequila Sunrises than I made per hour as president of my company.

In addition to the stories I have already related, I'll interject a couple more here that you may find amusing. The first one could be titled, "When the cat is away, the mice will play."

Because of my personal knowledge from working in restaurants in college, I was aware of what sometimes goes on in restaurants after closing. My restaurants all had burglar alarm systems designed to alert the burglar alarm company of irregularities. Each night at closing, the manager would set the alarm and the time would be noted at the burglar alarm company. I had requested (unbeknown to the restaurant manager) that the alarm company send me a list of the closing times each month. I began to notice a tendency of very late closing times (normally on Friday or Saturday) at the Hungry Dutchman. I decided to investigate. On the following Friday night, I set my alarm for three A.M. When I drove into the Hungry Dutchman parking lot, I almost had a heart attack. On each arm of the revolving, giant, five-story windmill rode one of my employees. The party ended a few moments later with my arrival. Needless to say, the Hungry Dutchman had a new GM the following day.

The second story should be titled, "Avoiding an embarrassing moment." This incident took place at the Broker. I was helping out at the restaurant on a busy Saturday night by working the reservation desk. A well-dressed and very confident gentleman approached the reservation desk. When I asked if he had a reservation, he proceeded to tell me that he was a personal friend of Tom Wilscam and that Tom had advised him to use his name and he would be assured of immediate seating. After a moment of amused reflection, I decided on the following course of action; I told the man that I would be happy to honor Mr. Wilscam's courtesy to him, but since it was a company policy that all customers are to be treated equally, I would have to call Mr. Wilscam to get permission to break that policy. The gentleman, whose manner was previously very confident, immediately became a bit more humble. He told me that no, he would not want to bother Mr. Wilscam at home and that he and his party would have a drink in the lounge and asked that I do my best on getting them a table.

I love relating these stories because very few paying jobs offer the flip side of the restaurant business, that is, FUN (if you have a sense of humor), and certainly never a dull moment.

Another story, related to marketing, took place at the original Hungry Farmer in Denver: I was invited to attend the auction of the Grand Champion at the annual Denver Stock Show by Sonny Mappelli, the owner of the meat company who supplied our beef products. The bidding for the Grand Champion narrowed down to the two largest hotels in Denver. When I asked Sonny what they would do with the animal, he said that they would have it slaughtered and then advertise that they were serving prime Grand Champion beef. I had a flash of marketing inspiration and told him to enter the bidding on my behalf. As it turned out, I won. Now what to do with a megaton steer on my hands?

I placed a call to the Hungry Farmer maintenance man, and asked him to build a pen in front of the barn strong enough to hold a T-Rex, then called a friend in the advertising business and asked if he could get a story with heart in the local media. "What story," he asked. I told him I had gone to the Stock Show auction, and when I realized the fate that awaited the Grand Champion steer, I figured he deserved better. So I bought the prize hunk of beef for a pet, and kept him at the Hungry Farmer in the newly built pen at the front of the restaurant!

Everyone at the restaurant was ready to have me fitted for a straight jacket and committed to the nearest asylum, but were ecstatic when the story quickly made the rounds on every newspaper and TV news channel in the city. I would venture to say we received at least $100,000 worth of free publicity from my impulsive, thinking outside of the box idea. Because of the free media blitz, a constant crowd of people stopped by to see this magnificent piece of beef that I had saved from the slaughter house.

I can't remember if we named the Grand Champion, but he became known as GC for short. Each day around noon, a bus person would feed and groom GC. One bus person would then walk GC around the parking lot for his daily exercise. One day when there was a particularly large crowd of people, I decided I would show off a bit by walking GC myself. I was dressed in a suit and tie, ready for work that evening. As we circled the parking lot, GC began to quicken his pace. My efforts at trying to restrain him had little effect.

GC headed for an adjacent vacant field west of the restaurant. As he picked up speed, my feet were barely touching the ground as I clutched tightly to the rope. When we reached Wadsworth Street, approximately a quarter-mile away, GC began to slow his pace. However, we were now in the middle of busy street. Cars began swerving right and left to avoid a head on collision (a car, no doubt, would receive the worst of it). Fortunately, there were no accidents and eventually GC ran out of gas and I was able to lead him meekly back to his pen at the Hungry Farmer. A motorist did manage to get some pictures of this bizarre scene and we were all over the news again.

As a result of this episode I was informed by my insurance agent that it might not be a good idea to continue the practice of trying to exercise GC. We decided it was time for GC to receive his Grand Champion status reward in animal heaven. We donated him to the Wallace Home for Children, where they enjoyed servings of prime beef for many weeks.

Once your business is established, a limited amount of reminder advertising is good and should be done. Remember, you want to keep your name in front of your market to remind them to *come again.* Additionally, your market will be constantly evolving and changing.

New potential customers will be moving in and others leaving. Typically, an advertising budget of 2% of gross sales is recommended.

Giving away food or liquor may not at first sound like a cost-effective way to do business. However, it can be the most lucrative and
inexpensive marketing you can do. All investment of time and money
can only be judged by the results. By doing the unusual, you catch the
public's attention. Take for instance Denny's Restaurants' newest marketing campaign, advertised during the 2010 Super Bowl. Denny's
offered one full day of a free Grand Slam breakfasts. Think about how
many millions of people saw the ad, and how many new customers
went to Denny's because of this outrageous offer of free food for a
day. This approach is a little different than the standard "buy one and
get one free" or "with this coupon receive 10% off." Which do you
think would be more effective in bringing people in for the first time
and then back again?

Here are some standard, and perhaps not-so-standard marketing
ideas that can be effective when used at the right time and place:

Comment Cards: Have comment cards in the customer area, usually
near the entrance, to be filled out and left with the cashier. Include a
space for your customer's name and address, so you can mail special
offers to them: effective direct marketing. Comment cards often tell
you what the customer may be seeing that you don't. Do not overreact
to every negative comment. You cannot please everyone, so don't
even try. When negative comments are repeated, however, they should
be addressed, and changes considered. Specific comments about staff
attitude, cleanliness, ambience, menu items, and service should be
seriously considered. Others that imply that your whole restaurant is
lousy are ones you can do little about. Don't let them stick in your
craw; maybe the customer was having a bad day.

Register for Birthdays: Put a book in front of the cash register for customers to enter their email addresses. A sign above the book should
state, "May we send you a gift on your birthday? Enter you email
address." This will give you a database that not only reminds you to
send a birthday greeting and a gift certificate, but also enables you to
send your customers special announcements. Not only are these
effective public relations, but a birthday guest will seldom come
alone, thereby adding additional customers to your customer count.

VIP Club: Place a fish bowl on the counter with a sign asking customers to leave a business card and receive a membership in the restau-

rant's VIP club. Each month the cards are taken from the bowl and an email sent, announcing that, as a new member of the VIP club, they are entitled to a free lunch or dinner for two. A database is created and each month members receive a special offer of the month, be it a free cocktail, appetizer, or dessert, with an announcement of a special event.

The program has several obvious advantages:

- Creates a loyal customer base
- Extremely inexpensive reminder advertising
- Customers typically spend more when receiving something free
- Customer often invites a guest to dine with them when one or two of the meals are free

Frequently cited reasons for sales increases and profitability due to advertising are:

- More marketing to existing customers
- Loyalty/ frequent dining programs
- Monthly customer newsletter
- Social networking, for example, email

The common thread in these activities is that they give customers more reasons for putting the restaurant on their short list for dining.

Get a website up and running with an email distribution system: Have *Internet Only* specials that can be printed from your website. These coupons cost you little to produce and distribute to your customers, but can increase your repeat business.

Set up a Twittering program: There are over 283 million cell phones in the United States, according to Mobile Marketing Association (MMA), with over 95% of these cell phones capable of sending and receiving test messages. Most people have a cell phone with them all the time. A key to effective marketing is convenience. By providing cell or mobile phone ordering, customer convenience is taken to another level. There are several mobile marketing companies that provide cell phone or mobile phone ordering.

Currently, industry leaders like McDonalds, Burger King, Subway, and Pizza Hut are using cell or mobile phones to order burgers and pizza. Twitter messages can also be sent out announcing specials, promotions, and menu information.

If they don't come to you, go to them: Visit local businesses and drop off fax order forms and your catering menu to hospitals and pharmaceutical companies in your area. Offer a discount to salesmen on orders of $25.00 or more. Salesmen meet frequently with doctors and hospital staffs to introduce new products. Typically, the salesman will provide refreshments for the group. Run an ad in local high school and college papers—offer discounts to students with a student ID. Often, teachers will not have time or will prefer not to leave the teachers' lounge. Offering to deliver might be an appealing option for them.

Get your Staff Involved: Stamp the back of your business cards with employee names, and run a contest among your employees. The employee with the most business cards turned in with his/her name on the back over a given time-period gets a prize. Give a bonus prize of at least $100.00 cash or comparable value prize.

A fun idea that creates a buzz and increases business on a slow day is a roulette wheel at the cashier counter. (This is most applicable for a fast-food or fast-casual concept.) After the customer has placed their order and received their food, they would spin the wheel. Each slot on the wheel is designated for a percent discount, from 0% to 100% off, for their next visit to the restaurant.

In anticipation of the slow months of the year, Chili's customers receive from the manager a *Perfect Play* scratch card. The manager explains that the customer can redeem their prize in the designated month. Prizes range from a free Coke to $50 cash, and Chili's reports that it is one of their most effective promotions.

Promotional Idea Rewards: Create or, better yet, have your managers create a contest; whoever comes up with the best and most profitable or responsive promotional idea gets a prize at the end of the quarter. Be sure to set parameters that clearly measure this. For instance, you can measure the effectiveness of an idea by the volume it creates, like the gross number of guests generated or the dollars returned on your initial investment; for example, $100 initial cost yields $1000 dollars in sales, or 900% ROI (return on investment).

Mothers Day and Valentine's Day: These are two of the busiest days of the year for many restaurants. Take advantage of the fact that it is a sellers' market on those days and reach out to those customers who are looking for a good choice by the use of some of the selective marketing tips offered in this section.

Wholesale Accounts: Visit hotels, corporate cafeterias, schools, bed & breakfast establishments, golf courses, etc. Get creative; many businesses may be interested in wholesale costs of any specialty products you may have. I strongly suggest you do not offer credit terms. Because of accounting considerations, many corporate accounts will insist on credit terms. If the account is large enough, arrange with their accounting office to pay you in advance with a debit account. Typically, restaurants will have credit terms of fourteen days with their vendors. If the restaurant has accounts receivable of thirty or more days, it can produce a severe financial strain.

Community Events: Sponsor local youth and high school sports teams. Always measure the bang for your buck two ways: return on investment in dollars, and the goodwill you've generated.

Local Clubs: Book clubs, social clubs, wine clubs, etc.—and offer to host events during restaurant off-hours. Charge a nominal fee for space if they are not planning on food and beverage. If they are planning a menu, offer a full meal or light snacks, and do not charge for space.

Print Flyers: These can be handed out in parking lots and posted on bulletin boards throughout your market community; think libraries, grocery stores, health clubs, etc.

Send Direct Mailers: These are normally post cards with coupons, using zip codes for your market area only. Be aggressive and creative with your offer or your mailer will be tossed in the nearest wastebasket.

Post Coupons: These can be inserted in local mailers, such as *Val Pak* or any other coupon books. Again, be aggressive with your offer.

Ads in Local Papers: School or community papers, etc. may be relatively inexpensive and reach your local market. Offer a *get acquainted* deal.

Catering: If your restaurant is close to downtown, you'll find many government, bank, and office buildings ripe for aggressive marketing: catering for breakfast meetings, lunch meetings, and special events, for example. You can even hire a catering sales manager to sell and service these accounts, which can be lucrative. Set up a database with prospective companies to call on, as well as keep a record of current catering clients to send reminder flyers to.

Gift Certificates: These are a terrific way to increase sales. Holidays are obviously a great time to sell gift certificates. In-store table tents, signs, newsletters, (VIP club members), and Twitter are all inexpensive and effective ways to market your gift certificates. Back-to-school time is a great opportunity to sell a gift certificate to moms to give to their children instead of lunch cash, to make sure they are spending the money on a proper lunch.

Be aggressive with the gift certificate discount because, on average, 18% to 20% of gift certificates are never redeemed.

Coupon Discounting: This can be good and it can be bad. Subway turned their $5.00 foot-long into a national phenomenon. The success of the $5.00 foot-long raised Subway's sales by 17% last year, according to NPD Group.

On the other hand, the National Restaurant Association, in a survey of independent operators, reported the following: When asked what was the most effective change they had made last year to increase net income, rarely did anyone cite the use of discounts or coupons. Conversely, it was noted from operator's responses that more discounting or lowered prices resulted in a decline in net income.

Those operators who were seeing improved profits most frequently identified menu modification (not discounting), enhanced focus on customer service, improved cost controls, better buying practices, employee scheduling, and effective marketing as the reasons for improved profit.

Discounting food as *value meals* without also changing your portion size or the quality of the offering is a mistake because it emphasizes an already besieged value offer. When you reduce prices in this way, it tells the customer loud and clear that you were over-priced. At the same time, an increase in prices without added value is also a mistake.

Clearly, you must fit the marketing tips offered here to your restaurant concept. What may work most effectively for a fast-food or fast-casual restaurant may not work for a sit-down full service restaurant. One thing that will work for all restaurants is word-of-mouth advertising, and the only successful marketing technique to achieve positive word-of-mouth advertising is excellence in food, atmosphere, and service.

LOCATION, LOCATION, LOCATION

The significance of your location to the restaurant category and concept you have chosen cannot be overemphasized. The demographics in your business plan should match the profile of your target market, and the number of people that fit that profile should live within a one-to five-mile radius of your location.

Daytime employment will obviously be important if you plan on being open for breakfast and lunch. If you are open for dinner, you will need a fairly substantial residential population to sustain your business. For breakfast/lunch business, a high density office or retail area is necessary. Parking, visibility, and easy access should be prime factors when considering your location.

The one—three—five mile demographics will vary in importance depending on your location. The more urban an area is, the more traffic there will be, and the less distance potential customers will have to drive. Your market will most likely be within a one-to three-mile radius of your restaurant. A rural area will draw from a wider distance, of five miles or more.

Be careful in your evaluation of demographics. For example, the traffic count in front of your location may be a very large one, indicating great potential for drive-by business. However, the traffic demographics may be deceiving. They will tell you how many cars in a twenty-four-hour period drive by, but they will not tell you some things that only your physical observation will. How fast is the traffic going? Traffic that is too heavy, or cars driving fast, can be as bad as no traffic at all. Are there so many cars that access to your location may be difficult? What about visibility?

Traffic counts are more important to your success if you are a fast-food owner/operator, as opposed to someone who favors a classier, high-end, sit-down destination restaurant.

A year or two back, my company had a franchisee in New Jersey who was looking for a location for his first restaurant. I had provided him and his realtor with site criteria to help facilitate their search. One day, I received a call from the franchisee stating that he had two possible locations that he felt would work. They both had positive aspects that appealed to him, but he was uncertain about which one would be best. He felt that location A had much better demographics (a stronger, more reliable customer base) than location B. However, location A had more restaurant competition and a higher rent factor. Location B, on the other hand, had little competition and lower rent. But, the demographics were not as good as location A. Which should he consider? My answer was that the probable reason there was little competition at location B was because of the poor demographics.

"Why would you want to be somewhere where no one else wants to be?" I asked.

Additionally, rent will often correspond to the viability of the location. "The better the location, the higher the rent" is a pretty good rule of thumb. Remember, rent is relative to your sales volume. No matter what the rent is, 10% or less of gross sales is essential for an acceptable net profit.

OWNERSHIP

Ownership can be complex or simple. *Keep it simple,* is my mantra. Why clutter your dream restaurant with multiple owners? If, for economic reasons, you find it necessary to have business partners who will be involved in management, then make sure one person is in charge and overseeing all major decisions. Assign specific responsibilities to each partner according to their experience and talents. If responsibilities are not clearly defined, there is likely to be confusion and disagreement among the partners. The bottom line on the profit and loss statement is your barometer for success or failure. With each partner focusing on a specific part of the whole, your opportunity for success will improve. Each partner should be held specifically accountable for his or her area of responsibility, instead of everyone in management pointing fingers at one another when general problems arise.

If it's a multi-ownership business, all should agree to let the owner with the most experience manage or oversee management of the restaurant while the other partners diplomatically step back and let the chosen one manage without interference. If the partners cannot give their unconditional support to the owner/manager they select, then they have chosen the wrong person, and it's back to square one. Trying to control or change your original owner/manager's faulty ideas will only result in disagreement and turmoil. Nip this in the bud.

Remember the statistics from the National Restaurant Association: 82% of start-ups with no restaurant management experience will fail within the first year. They fail because they don't know what they don't know. Therefore, make sure your managing partner has the necessary management experience plus the motivation and business acumen to run the restaurant; if not, hire a professional restaurant manager to do the job.

Few restaurant owners want to spend all their time managing their restaurant unless it was their plan all along to create a job for themselves and be happy with the necessary hours involved. However, sooner or later, even the most devoted owner/manager will want to take more time off. There is one thing that I am very sure of in this life and that is that you cannot establish or maintain a successful restaurant without good management. As with all employees, finding a good manager begins with the right selection, and ends with meticulous training.

I once was interviewed by a national restaurant trade magazine. They were doing an article on restaurant manager training programs. The writer who interviewed me stated that they had heard there were over a dozen or so former managers of mine who had gone on to own and operate their own restaurants. When I confirmed that I thought that was true, the interviewer stated that I must have a very good management training program. I responded that I felt it was comprehensive but probably not much different than most other training programs. However, I thought there might be one significant difference and that was that I never hired anyone for management who I thought would be happy being a manager for the rest of their lives. If they told me that they wanted my job, I would hire them on the spot.

If a person has ambition, initiative, and the fortitude to set a goal with a plan and stick to it, they will succeed. I typically would make a deal with a new prospective manager. If they turned out to be as good as I thought they could be and stayed with me for five years or more, I would do all I could to help them get into business for themselves. This was a win/win deal and, for the most part, worked out well.

Once you have selected the right person and trained them at length, there can still be problems if your specific management objectives are not clearly communicated and understood. In other words, are you both on the same page about your expectations? One of the very best tools that I have found to accomplish this is MBO (Management by Objective).

A Management by Objective Management Compensation Plan

MBO is an old and proven management system that has been emulated many times over by modern day business gurus such as Covey, Drucker, and many others less well known. The principle is simple: accountability through agreed-to expectations.

The objective is written by you and your general manager. The objective must be specific, stretching, and with a completion date. Most importantly, it must be agreed to by you and your GM with complete understanding and no ambiguity.

Due to the broad nature of some objectives, which can cause some ambiguity, a second part to the objective is written, called, "By that I mean." In this section, point-by-point clarified explanations are listed until both you and your GM agree on expectations.

This plan is based on the principle of extra financial incentive through specific, achieved goals and appropriate rewards. It has the additional advantage of ensuring long-term employment by making the GM feel more a partner than just an employee.

1. Base salary of approximately $$K. May vary in certain geographical areas.

2. A quarterly bonus based on four equal parts: gross sales volume, food cost, labor cost, and QE (quality evaluation) score. These are the operational factors that the GM can control. The net profit will be driven by these four categories. Designed as follows:

Ownership and the GM sit down at the end of each quarter and write an objective for each of the above categories for the following quarter. The written objective must be specific, measurable, and stretching. It must be agreed to by both of you as reasonable. A sample objective is as follows: Sales for 2nd quarter 2005 will be not less than $60,000 (keep in mind number of days in month and seasonal factors). Food cost will not exceed 30% and labor cost will not exceed 26% (volume will effect labor %). Quarterly QE score will be 90 or above. All line items on P&L, for example, legal, accounting, repairs, etc. should be agreed upon and set with a specific budget.

Ownership will use the objective as a barometer for the bonus, but it will be somewhat subjective. Ownership may decide that the objectives were not met without fault of the GM and give the bonus or a portion of it anyway. However, make sure that the negative circumstances were severe enough to justify giving ground and that it does not become a habit or the written objective will lose its power.

1. In the 1st two quarters of operation in the 1st year, you will have some expenses that would not be normal to regular operations. Therefore, this period of time would be used to establish realistic objectives that both you and your GM can agree on. No bonus would be paid during this period.

2. If all objectives were met in the 3rd quarter, then the GM would receive a 5% bonus of net profit for that quarter in addition to base salary. The same would apply to the 4th quarter.

3. The 2nd year would be based on 10% bonus per quarter. The 3rd year, if all quarter objectives were met the previous year, would be 15%; 4th year, 20%; 5th and subsequent years, 25%. The GM would not proceed to the next bonus level for the following year unless quarterly objectives were met all four quarters of the previous year. He/she basically becomes your 25% partner. However, if they leave your employment, they of course forfeit all benefits. Insurance and other benefits are optional, depending on your bottom line and how much you value your GM.

This plan may seem financially aggressive but the store's profits are directly related to the GM's performance. The more he/she makes in bonus, the more you will make.

Variations in bonus compensation can be made to the plan. However, the basic premise of specific and agreed-to accountability is essential.

MANAGEMENT

First, identify the key positions for your chosen category of restaurant. A fast-food or fast-casual outlet will typically have a general manager, an assistant manager, and possibly one or two hourly shift supervisors. Conversely, with a chic, fine-dining restaurant, in addition to a GM and possibly two assistant managers, you will need a chef and possibly a sous-chef or pastry chef (if you are making your own breads, desserts, etc.). Management requirements for the different categories vary widely.

You will need to establish what work qualifications you require for your management positions. Work experience is obviously important, but equally important are the personalities of your managers. It is essential that general managers in any restaurant be pleasant, knowledgeable, and flexible, regardless of restaurant concept, because they will be dealing with staff as well as customers. In hiring a GM, make sure the person you choose has successfully demonstrated reliability and trustworthiness in their prior employments—watch for these traits on their resumes.

Work history can be obtained by checking references with previous employers. Many employers may be reluctant to give you more information other than dates of employment. Try to talk directly to department supervisors on a personal level. Tell them you are fully aware that they must be diplomatic about volunteering information because of potential liability issues, then ask if they could just answer "yes" or "no" to your pertinent questions.

Equally important as the reference check is how you perceive your new GM. I have my own perspective; to me, a good GM is akin to a good athletic coach. Do they have an aura of leadership and can they communicate well? Are they enthusiastic about their profession and confident in their abilities? Can they put together and lead a winning team? In my case, the answer had to be a resounding yes to each question, or I wouldn't hire them.

The following personal experience is an example of just how important a reference check is to hiring the right person for a key position. This happened at a time when I owned and operated multiple restaurants. We had unexpectedly lost an executive chef at one of our high-end restaurants. Needless to say, a gourmet restaurant without a chef can be a significant problem. The manager was temporally filling that position, and most anxious to find a new executive chef.

One day, the manager called me with good news; he was sure we had an applicant whose resume looked perfect for the position. I asked if he had checked his references. He replied that he had not because of his perceived urgency of filling the position immediately. I insisted that he check the references before proceeding any further. As it turned out, the resume was a complete fabrication and our new executive chef had actually been in prison for the past twelve years. I would not be opposed to giving a person, warts and all, a new start if I felt they were sincere. However, falsifying a resume was not the best sign of turning over a new leaf; honesty is one trait I absolutely demand in an employee, as should you.

The restaurant business is really a people business—bottom line. Management must demonstrate leadership by not only being outgoing and accommodating to customers, but by being able to communicate well with staff. A leader who is a true professional teaches by example as well as training employees with skill and patience. If service is important to the GM, it will become important to the staff. If cleanliness is a priority to the GM, it will become so with the staff. An old saying in the industry is, "If you go into a restaurant and see a lot of long-faced employees, look for the one with the longest face: that will be the general manager." In my fifty years in the restaurant business, I have never seen a successful restaurant with a bad general manager. As with any other business, success or failure begins and ends with good management.

A professionally run restaurant depends on operations manuals to provide policy, job procedures, and operational instructions so that management and staff can maintain a consistent and positive experience for the restaurant's customers. Managing a restaurant can be stated simply: "Management runs the system, and the system runs the restaurant."

OPERATIONAL SYSTEMS

Operational systems are the navigational instruments and the rudder of a great ship. They set the course and steer the ship on a straight and smooth course. Proven operational systems must be provided in order for the restaurant team to function successfully. Operational systems not only provide a designated way to perform the job, but they maintain and assure a continuity of excellence.

In the simplest definition, operational systems are those methodologies used to perform the many functions of the restaurant. However, there are a multitude of functions that must be *systematized*, ranging from human resource functions to production functions to service functions. Essentially, you are defining "how do I do these tasks?" in a way that's effective, consistent, and legal and ethical. So, first you must create the systems; then you must formalize the systems you've created in written manuals; then you must train your staff to follow these systems. Your training program, in and of itself, is an operational system. I recommend having three manuals, as follow:

- Managers' Operations Manual
- Company Policy Manual
- Employee Operations Manual

I will elaborate on how to lay out each of these manuals.

Managers' Operations Manual (MOM)

This manual is for the benefit of the management team and provides direction from ownership about how the business should be conducted. You, as an owner, should meet with every manager and go through this manual. It should include the following sections:

I. Ownership Structure

Here you should tell your managers exactly who they're working for. Ensure that they understand the company structure and the company's mission statement. If there are other owners (partners) that frequent the business but are not active, make sure your managers, and your partners, understand the extent of their authority.

II. Authority of Managers

Define the limits of authority of managers: who can hire, who can fire, who handles banking, etc. The best way to do this is to formally delineate your various management position job descriptions so that each management team member understands the scope and limits of their authority.

III. Management's Duty to Ownership

First and foremost, I always impress upon managers that their primary responsibility is to *manage the cash*. Make it clear that mismanagement of the money (lost cash drawers, lost deposits, unlocked offices and safes, frivolous comps, etc.) is a deal breaker between you and them.

Managers must agree to support and enforce the policies of the company, as spelled out in the Employee Policy Manual. It is extremely important to make it clear that managers' loyalty must be to the company first and foremost, not to employees or any other causes they may tend to embrace.

This is where you, as the owner, provide your definition of management and clearly define your expectations: a certain level of profit, a certain company culture, an expectation of supporting ownership's interests, what your expectation and definition of management is.

Here's one I use: "Management is responsible for creating and maintaining a safe, productive, and motivational environment within the work place."

However you define it, there are several key words in this description that should be stressed:

- Responsibility: Management accepts complete responsibility for the success or failure of the restaurant. While a good manager can, and must, delegate responsibilities to employees, he or she must never abdicate these responsibilities.
- Creating and Maintaining a Good Work Environment: This does not happen by chance; it must be created and maintained. This goes to a popular concept called "Company Culture." Good management is sensitive to what approaches work best for their type of staff. Most restaurant workers are temporary and tend to be in a younger age group. The younger age groups today don't respond well to dictatorial styles of management. As long as poli-

cies and procedures are clearly stated, they will generally perform. But they perform better when they are given a level of empowerment, be it through contributing ideas to improve service or efficiencies, being allowed to resolve customer complaints, etc. Because of their contemporary upbringing, they respond better to positive reinforcement than negative reinforcement such as harsh criticism or demerits.

- Safe: Employees must feel safe, both physically and emotionally. Physical safety can be attained by providing them tools they need to ensure safe procedures; for example, fryer filtering equipment versus filtering by hand; or non-slip shoes to prevent slips and falls in the kitchen. Emotional safety is attained by building a culture that is based on positive reinforcement, fair and consistent treatment of everyone, and an environment free of harassment.

- Productive: Employees want to feel productive. They don't want to feel that their efforts are pointless. Feeling productive and understanding that they are an integral part of a team will help keep employees on task and make the job of management much easier.

- Motivational Environment: Management must encourage a culture that is motivational. This is a skill that separates great managers from average managers. By providing goals—service goals, sales goals, or cost goals—that are realistic and attainable, a much more positive attitude among the staff as a whole will be accomplished. Managers must recognize and reward employees who reach goals, even if the reward is merely recognizing them and giving them positive reinforcement. Those employees who respond exceptionally well should be given more responsibility and be considered for supervisory positions.

IV. Human Resources

In this section of the Managers' Operations Manual, you dictate the process of hiring, training, and disciplining that you want employed in your restaurant operation.

Hiring: Emphasize that State and Federal labor laws must be adhered to. Review those guidelines, such as minimum wage, breaks, minors, etc., right from the posters that you're required to display. State in the Manual how hiring should be conducted, answering these questions:

a. How will you "source" your staff? Craigslist, newspaper, employment agencies, "Now hiring" signs, etc.?

b. Who will interview prospective employees? Will it be the owner or general manager, department heads (kitchen manager for kitchen workers, dining room manager for front-of-the-house staff)? What is your policy of reference checking or running background checks? Who makes the final call? If you as the owner are active in the business, I recommend that you make the final call, or at least have a say in the process. After all, your staff is your most valuable asset. Naturally, you should be sensitive to the recommendations of your management team.

c. Where is employee information kept? A file should be opened for each employee that will contain their employment application, W-4, I-9 (and any other required federal forms), their signed Employee Policy Manual acknowledgement form, and perhaps their signed uniform agreement. This folder will collect all subsequent individual paperwork including warnings, certifications, performance appraisals, etc.

d. Wage determination: Make sure that the employee is clear as to what his or her starting wage is, *before* they report for their first shift. It is sloppy procedure to not be in agreement on this issue after a job offer is made. Write the agreed-upon wage on the application and have the new employee initial it.

e. Training schedule: New employees are always nervous and unsure. Managers should make it very clear what their training schedule will be and when the new employee will be expected to be ready to handle shifts on their own.

Training: Here is where you define what your training system generally looks like. It should be clearly laid out, consistent, and include documentation such as quizzes, acknowledgements, certification tests, and service checks (evaluations of them on the job). While chain restaurants and franchises almost always have elaborate training programs, your program may be scaled down to a level that's appropriate for your projected sales volume. In any event, it should always encompass the following steps:

a. New Employee Training: Establish in your MOM that this can be done either individually or in small groups and should be conducted by a veteran manager, be it the GM, a training manager, or an experienced assistant manager. The specifics of the new employee orientation are addressed in more detail in the following section, the Employee Operations Manual.

b. Job Position Training: What is your system for training employees to be competent in their specific job position? Will you rely primarily on on-the-job-training? Will you devote a specific person to be in charge of all training? Will you designate key people within departments (kitchen, dining room, or bar) who are deemed *trainers*. To a large degree, your decision in this area must be based on the complexity of your operation. For example, if your wine list has sixty wines on it, you need to have a way to effectively train your servers to know at least a little bit about each one. Specific job position training is addressed in detail in the Employee Operations Manual.

c. Ongoing Training: It is said that training never ends. Whether or not you have a formal ongoing training program in place, offering employees continual feedback and training is a win/win proposition. It enhances their performance and keeps them motivated, knowing that management is committed to their constant improvement of job performance. Ongoing training can come in many forms; perhaps you select your best employees and send them to tradeshows or workshops; bring in experts on site, for example a wine expert, and have an after-or before-hours seminar. I recommend the use of performance appraisals as a form of ongoing training. To effectively do this, you must commit to a time period, perhaps annually or bi-annually, where a manager sits down with each employee and gives them feedback on their performance. It is a great opportunity to listen to them, as well, and get them to recommit to certain goals and objectives. I recommend cross-training employees as much as possible. The more flexible you are with your staff's job positions, the easier your shift scheduling will become.

Discipline: What is the process of discipline that you want your company to practice? It is extremely important to define the process, communicate it to your employees during orientation, and consistently practice it. It is every manager's responsibility to practice discipline objectively, whether they particularly like an employee or not. If staff understands that the process will be consistently and objectively applied, hard feelings will be minimized. I suggest this process:

- Verbal warnings: for minor first offenses. Remember, when being critical, criticize the behavior, not the person. For example, say to an employee, "You clearly chose not to bathe today and that's unacceptable," rather than, "You stink; go home and bathe."
- Written warnings: for major first offenses and repeat offenses. You should have a form with a section for the manager to chronicle the offense, a manager's signature line, an employee's signature line (they can refuse to sign), and a section where an employee can make a comment. These warnings go into the permanent employee file and are building blocks to easily end your relationship with them. Effective, generic *written warning* forms are available at office supply stores.
- Suspension: When a written warning has been issued, and an employee repeats an offense, suspension is an effective way to get their attention. I generally find that employees who earn suspensions are probably not going to make the grade, long term. Suspensions can range from taking away prime shifts, like weekends for servers, to being taken off the schedule completely for a period of time.
- Termination: Certain offenses are terminable upon first offense and these should be reviewed with employees during orientation; theft, harassment, violence, overt rudeness to customers, etc. are examples of possible first offense terminable offenses.

Here are some other guidelines for disciplining employees to list in the Managers' Operations Manual:

- It is important to be calm and never yell, or even raise your voice when disciplining an employee. If you're angry, it's better to wait until you calm down before addressing an issue.
- Be as specific as possible, using examples whenever possible. Again, focus on the behavior, not personality.
- Offer reasons for improving, and consequences for not improving.
- Make sure the employee knows exactly how to improve.
- Offer benchmarks and ways to measure improvement in the future.
- Once the discussion is over, leave it in the past. Never discuss it with other employees.

As a matter of policy for managers, disciplining employees should generally be done behind closed doors, and certainly not in front of other employees. If there is an adversarial relationship between a manager and an employee or, in cases where there is a gender difference between a manager and an employee, it is a good idea to have another manager present as a witness, especially when suspension or termination is likely to be the end result.

Workers' Compensation: As discussed earlier, one of management's responsibilities is to ensure a safe working environment. In spite of all the efforts made, employee injuries will occur. The most common injury in the restaurant business is the slip and fall. Wet floors are almost always the culprit. Management must continually have their eyes open to potential high risk conditions. These conditions can be mitigated through good design (non-slip treatments to floors) and maintenance practices (knife sharpening service, as sharp knives are actually safer than dull knives).

Most importantly in MOM is to address the procedure of dealing with employee injuries. Whatever procedures are described in the MOM must be consistently conveyed in the Employee Policy Manual and reiterated during new employee orientations. Coverage requirements may vary from state to state, but Workers' Compensation insurance is always required. Many states will allow employers to 'designate' a specific provider for on-the-job injuries. If this is the case, your Workers' Compensation insurance provider will require that the designated provider be used unless they approve another provider.

Be clear in your MOM what procedures should be followed. Stress to employees that *all* on-the-job injuries should be reported. It may be that minor first aid can be applied without further medical attention. When in doubt, managers should be instructed to err on the cautious side and send the injured employee in for medical attention. In the event that an emergency situation arises, for example a cook cuts their finger and it needs stitches, don't allow them to drive themselves to the emergency room; either drive them yourself or send them with a reliable employee. In such a case, both employees should be considered "on-the-clock" for the full duration of their scheduled shift.

V. Security

An important section in the MOM should deal with security procedures that are put in place and religiously practiced. This would include money counting procedures and bank deposits, office security, rules about exterior doors being locked at closing, and proper use of alarm and video security systems that are installed. Certain rules should always be in place:

- No manager or employee should be alone in the building at closing. At least two staff members should be present upon securing the building.
- Female staff should be escorted to their vehicles by a manager or another employee at night if high risk conditions exist.
- Money should be counted behind closed doors.
- Frequent cash drops (money removed from cash drawers and placed in the safe) should be made.
- Appropriate fire and burglar alarms are installed, maintained, and properly used.

VI. Crises/Disaster Situations

What separates managers from employees is that managers have to be able to deal with those rare but inevitable extraordinary situations. Examples may include:

- armed robbery
- severe injury or illness, (employee or customer)
- fatality (employee or customer)
- foodborne illness incident
- extreme weather
- riots or brawls

Here are some general guidelines, followed by some recommended responses to a few specific situations:

1. Be a leader: Stay calm and in control. Act quickly and decisively. Even when the situation is out of control around you, you must maintain your cool and objectively work toward regaining control of the situation.

2. Use the people around you: You'll know who can help you deal with these situations. Direct those people to specific tasks.

3. Seek help as soon as possible: Contact the owner as soon as it's feasible to do so. In certain situations, don't hesitate to call 911.

4. Avoid making statements to the press: Leave that for the general manager or owner.

Severe or Fatal Injury: Get the police, fire department, and medical personnel involved as soon as possible (dial 911). Have employees step in to control curious crowds and keep them some distance from the event. If you are trained, administer first aid such as CPR or stop severe bleeding. Protect yourself first! Do not expose yourself to HIV through someone's blood; always use gloves when administering first aid. Defer to a doctor or other medical person who might be readily available among customers.

Riot or Brawl: Call 911 immediately. Be clear with the dispatcher that the situation is potentially out of control and that more than one officer may be required. Announce to the rioting or brawling group that the police are on the way. NEVER step into the middle of a brawl. Use employees to keep curious customers separated from the group causing the problem.

Robbery: One of the most terrifying experiences a manager may have to endure is armed robbery. There are a few preventative steps that you should always take:

Ways to Avoid Being Robbed

- Never be alone when you're closing.
- Watch for suspicious-looking people, especially around closing time. Be especially concerned about people who appear to be *casing* the closing operation (studying patterns). If you are concerned about an individual or group, call 911 and request that police come by and do a walk-through.
- Don't count or flash money in front of customers.
- Lock the office door while you're counting and after you've counted.
- Lock the building doors while doing closing countdowns.
- Never leave the safe on "day lock." Always spin the dial.
- Assume that someone is preparing to rob you and practice top-level security such as locking doors, securing funds, etc.

If you are confronted with an individual who is armed, perhaps with a gun or knife, cooperate fully with their instructions. You're just one person, and only goal at that point is survival. Give them what they want as quickly as you can. Do not stall; if they are nervous, they are dangerous. Try to get a good look at them, but make it clear to them that you are no threat and intend to cooperate with their wishes. Don't worry about giving them the money. The business is insured for such incidents. If there are employees present, tell them to stay calm and cooperate. Once the perpetrators have left, call the police. Collect as much information as you can, such as physical descriptions, vehicle description, etc. Do not put yourself at risk. Contact the owner as soon as possible.

If you are approached outside the building after you have armed the burglar alarm and are told to go back inside, let the perpetrator know that the alarm has been set and will have to be disarmed. If they require you to do so, enter and disarm the system. Some alarm systems have a panic code component that will silently tip off the alarm monitoring company that an incident is in progress and they will contact local law enforcement.

Remember: In an armed robbery, trying to be a hero can be deadly. Survival is your primary goal. Cooperate. Let the police do their job.

VII. Procedural and Reporting Responsibilities

In this section of the Managers' Operations Manual, you tell your managers exactly what accounting tools you expect them to use to effectively manage the business. These may include the following:

- Daily Sales Report: Daily bank deposit procedures should be tied to this report.
- Daily or Weekly Labor Analysis: I recommend reconciling your labor cost on a daily basis. The point-of-sale systems used today make it easy to do.
- Physical Inventory: A formal counting and valuing of inventory on hand, be it daily, weekly or monthly, should be a part of reporting procedures. Accurate food costing cannot be done without an accurate inventory of products on hand.
- Weekly Prime Cost Report: This is a report that looks at both labor cost and food cost for the week and is tied to the classic 80/20 rule—80% of your costs are tied to 20% of your expense line items, that is, labor cost and food and beverage cost. When looking at labor cost, you include all associated costs, like payroll taxes, Workers' compensation insurance, and employee benefits. When looking at food and beverage cost, you adjust your amount of expenditures reflected by purchases by the increase or decrease in the value of your inventory. Your percentage goal for Prime Cost will depend on the type of service system you employ. If you're a fast-casual restaurant, Prime Cost should run between 55% and 60%. If you're a full service restaurant, prime cost

should run between 60% and 65%. Wherever you set the mark, a weekly analysis will ensure that you know how you're doing, well ahead of receiving financial statements from your accountant long after the end of your accounting period.

- Opening and Closing Checklists: These are very helpful, especially to newer managers, as a tool to ensure that every necessary task is performed prior to opening and after closing the restaurant.

- Managers' Logbook: I highly recommend the use of this tool. It's an efficient way for managers to communicate with each other. The nature of the communication can range from issues with employees to maintenance or equipment problems. For example, if the night manager has called for a repair of a refrigeration unit, it should be noted in the logbook so the day manager doesn't duplicate the call.

VIII. The "How To" Section

In this section you provide your management team with procedures to address their job responsibilities. Following is an example of the information that might be covered in this section of the MOM:

Food and Beverage Cost and Controls: Food and beverage cost control encompasses the following procedures:

- effective inventory management
- proper recipe costing
- ensuring that all sales are accounted for
- having effective security controls in place to ensure against theft

Food and beverage cost typically accounts for as much as 25% to 40% of restaurant revenue. Obviously, proper management of this cost is essential to ensuring a healthy bottom line. It is the company's responsibility to set menu pricing that allows food and beverage cost objectives to be attainable and to establish systems that management ensures are effectively used to reach these objectives.

Inventory Control

This involves assessing product usage on a daily basis and assessing a *par level* for each product. By par level, I mean how much of each product you use, on average, between your regular distributor shipments (usually par levels are established for en-e day periods).

Most modern Point of Sale (POS) systems have the capability to track product usage over a designated period of time. Managers should learn to use reports generated for the purpose as tools for setting par levels and generating purchase orders.

Occasionally, your vendors will not have a product available or you may have unusual sales of one particular product item. Make sure that you maintain proper stock levels to minimize the possibility of running out of any product. It is a good idea to order approximately 10% more than your previous week's usage and adjust with each order. Your customers will expect that you will be able to serve them all menu items at all times.

Detailing Inventory Monthly

Each month you will have a beginning inventory value and an ending inventory. To establish a true value of inventory on hand involves counting each and every case/package and loose product on hand. It is suggested that you take a monthly inventory at the end of the last day of the month or before business starts on the first day of the next month.

Food Cost Goals

Hitting food cost percentage goals is essential in the success and profitability of a restaurant. Management must measure food cost consistently and accurately.

An acceptable food cost percentage can range from 26% to 32% of your total sales, depending on the market in which the restaurant is located. Anything over a 32% food cost, however, will start to cut away at your bottom line and decrease profits.

Calculating Food Cost

Your food cost is a measure of how much you spend on a product versus the price that you sell it for. Food cost is measured over a period of time, a week, month, or year. Here is the procedure to calculate food cost percentage:

1. Establish the value of your beginning and ending inventories for the period being addressed. Be sure that you extend the dollar value of each product based on the correct unit price. For example, if you paid $20 for a *case* of tomatoes, *don't* extend the *number of tomatoes* you have on hand by $20; that would dramatically overstate the value of your tomato inventory. In some cases, you will have to estimate how much is left in a bag or case. In this case, round to the nearest quarter of a unit.

2. Determine your inventory variation. Beginning inventory value minus ending inventory value = inventory variation (BI—EI = IV). Note: If the ending inventory value is higher than your beginning value, your inventory variation will be a negative number, which becomes essentially a credit against purchases made during that period.

3. Add your inventory variation to your total purchases for the period to get the true cost of what was used.

4. Divide the true cost of what was used by the total sales during the period.

5. The result will be your food cost percentage.

6. Calculating your liquor cost works exactly the same way.

For example:

1. On the first of the month we take an inventory of all the food in the restaurant. From that inventory, we calculate the dollar value as $5,500. Thus, our beginning inventory is $5,500.

2. After close on the last day of the month, take an inventory of all the food in the restaurant. This becomes the ending inventory. Let's say its $2,000.

3. Establish your Inventory Variation (BI—EI = IV) = $3,500

4. Add the total of food invoices received for the month. In this example, that total is $8,000.

5. Establish Total Sales for the month. Let's say that number is $35,000.

Here's how the calculation would run.
For example:

Inventory Variation	$3,500
+ Purchases	$8,000
Total Food Used	$11,500
÷ Net Sales	$35,000
=	.329
Or expressed in %	32.9%

Receiving:

The first step to managing inventory is receiving inventory. The manager on duty (MOD) should always receive any shipment of inventory. There are three steps to receiving inventory:

- Inspect it. Products that are not in good condition (bent cans, broken seals, etc.) should be refused.
- Check it against your original order sheet to ensure that the product, size, and quantity match.
- Store it in the proper place, ensuring that the older product is in front of new product (FIFO—first in, first out).

Invoice Handling

It is important to keep track of every invoice you receive. Further, it is imperative that costs are properly categorized; for example, if you code paper plates to food cost when it should have gone to supply cost, you are overstating the cost of food, which will overstate your food cost percentage.

Reasons for High Food Costs

If your food-costs are too high, these are the areas you should take a close look at:

- Product Pricing: You must monitor any changes in pricing from your vendors and adjust accordingly. There is restaurant-specific accounting software that will alert you to increases in pricing on invoice entry.
- Waste and Portion Control: Monitor portioning closely, ensuring that all recipes are being followed according to portions and procedures. Ensure that your food inventory is being properly rotated and properly dated according to established procedures to avoid spoilage.
- Accounting Errors: Double-check invoices and daily deposits to make sure there are no mistakes. Look for credits or shortages that may have been missed. Check your inventory calculations for errors. Re-count restaurant inventory if necessary. Go back and reprint all reports, and look at daily sales records to find any possible omissions or mistakes. Check cashier logs for shortages on a regular basis.
- Theft: Your final, and unfortunately most likely, reason for high food costs is theft. Theft can occur in many forms, from blatant theft of money or product to a cashier not ringing in sales for

friends, co-workers, or big tippers. Theft control is greatly enhanced by letting your staff know you're watching for it. The use of video surveillance is effective. Employees who are prone to steal will rationalize the theft in any number of ways. The following procedures should always be in force:

– Cash drawer accountability: only one cashier to each cash drawer
– Sales voids by managers only
– Constant inventory monitoring, especially on high cost items and alcohol inventory
– Back door security: it should be locked and or monitored at all times
– Use secret shoppers who not only look for food and service quality, but watch for questionable employee practices

Placing a Product Order

Each distributor has an order day and a delivery day. Before placing an order, first take an inventory to see what you have on-hand. Those who place orders must be skilled in knowing usage trends and have an idea of the expected sales volume for the period between orders.

Many POS systems on the market will actually generate purchase orders based on the sales that have gone through the system. This is called *perpetual inventory*. While it is an excellent tool for management use, nothing replaces a physical inventory count. A comparison of book inventory value, the inventory value that your POS system reports, versus your actual physical inventory value will quickly reveal problem areas.

Labor Cost and Controls

Labor costs will amount to the second highest expense category, behind food and beverage cost. Between the two of them, (Prime Cost), your financial success or failure will be determined. Labor cost is defined as the combined cost of the following expenses:

• Salaries and hourly wages
• Payroll taxes: Employers are required to match employee contributions to the Social Security fund at a rate of 6.2% of wages up to $106,800 in earnings (for 2010) and the Medicare fund at a rate of 1.45% of wages with no maximum. Additionally, employers must pay into both the federal and state unemployment funds,

typically up to a rate of 6.2% of wages up to a maximum determined by the state. The maximum is a function of the pressure on
the state fund from claims and can fluctuate.

- Workers' Compensation Insurance: This insurance is required by
  the state and covers on-the-job injuries that may occur. Rates are
  established based on the total projected salary and wages and are
  typically adjusted up or down based on the number and cost of
  claims made.

- Employee Benefits: These costs range from the cost of health
  insurance you may offer to certain employees to the cost of discounts or free meals that you provide.

Establishing your target labor cost is a process of building a schedule that effectively covers the anticipated staffing needs of your restaurant, establishing a wage structure and simply extending the
number of hours used by the hourly wages paid, and then adding fixed
salaries. Typically in the restaurant business, an acceptable labor cost
is between 25% to 30% of sales, including your management salaries.
Your labor cost percentage will be directly related to your sales volume. For every dollar you produce in sales, how much of that dollar
goes to paying your employees? While the labor cost goal is 25%, it
may range from 22% to 28%. As your sales volume increases, your
labor cost should go down as you optimize staff productivity. Conversely, as your sales volume decreases, your labor cost percentage
will increase.

Calculating Labor Cost

Your labor cost can be calculated for any period of time—a shift, a
day, week, month, or a year. To calculate labor cost, simply divide
total dollars paid in labor by the total sales for the period you are mea-
suring. Then multiply by 100 to get the percentage.

On the following page, you will find a sample Labor Cost Analysis
for a lunch shift.

As you can see, this labor cost percentage appears to be within our
acceptable range. However, this calculation does not take into account
a pro rata share of management salaries, payroll taxes, Workers'
Compensation costs, or employee benefits. Once those are added in,
you may well be out of the acceptable range. You must be aggressive
in managing your labor costs to keep them in line. For example, during slower than anticipated periods, send employees home early.
Skilled scheduling is a key component to labor cost control.

Employee	Hourly Wage	# Hours Worked	$ for Employee
Cashier	$9/hr	8 hrs	$72
Cashier #2	$8/hr	3 hrs	$24
Service Line	$10/hr	8 hrs	$80
Service Line #2	$9/hr	6 hrs	$54
Prep Person	$9/hr	7.5 hrs	$67.50
Dish Washer	$7.25	8hrs	$58
Food Runner	$8.00	5 hrs	$40
Total hourly wages			395.50
÷ Net Sales of $1500			0.26366
x 100			26.4%

Managing labor cost requires the MOD to be able to correctly ascertain proper staffing levels while always ensuring excellent customer service as the first priority.

Scheduling to Control Labor Cost

First, you must know what your target labor cost is. Then you must determine your Average Hourly Wage (AHW). To calculate this, add the hourly wage of all of your employees together and then divide that total by the total number of employees. In calculating AHW, it is reasonable to take management salaries and break them down to hourly rates and add them into the equation. The result will be your average hourly wage.

Once you've established your AHW, you then establish your projected sales for the period you are scheduling, typically a week. Historical data is the best source for projecting sales. If, for example, you are projecting $25,000 in sales for the week, and your target labor cost is 25%, then you have $6,250 to spend on labor ($25,000 X 25%). Dividing $6,250 by your AHW gives you the number of hours you have to schedule for the week. So, if your AHW in this example is $8.95, you have 698 hours available to build into your schedule ($6,250 ÷ $8.95).

Now that you know how many hours you have to fill with your hourly employees, you simply put them on the schedule where they fit best, making sure to avoid overtime when at all possible. Overtime will obviously affect your AHW for that week.

Reasons for High Labor Cost

If your labor cost percentage is rising consistently above the acceptable amount of 30%, here are a few things to look for:

- Your pricing structure may be too low to support your labor requirements.
- Your staff is not as productive as it could be.
- Scheduling is improper according to anticipated sales.
- Not enough employees are cross-trained, preventing the MOD from being able to send employees home on slower days.
- Control the AHW of employees. If your sales are not increasing, avoid wage increases.
- Inaccurate reporting of employees' hours: ensure that employees are clocking-out for breaks.
- Excessive overtime. Avoid it where possible.
- Make sure employees work according to scheduled hours. Do not allow employees to clock in more than ten minutes early, or hang around past their scheduled off time. These minutes will add up quickly.

Management should check labor costs daily; this is made easy by modern day POS systems with integrated timekeeping.

IX. Manager's Acknowledgement

Contracts, whether binding or not, are effective tools to reiterate the importance of a commitment. Each manager should sign an acknowledgement form for the company that reads as follows:

(Restaurant Name)_____

Manager Commitment Acknowledgement

I,_____, accept the position of _____Manager (Supervisor) of _____(Company Name). I hereby acknowledge that I have read the Managers' Operations Manual and understand and accept the contents therein.

Name_____

Date_____

Company Policy Manual (CPM)

The Company Policy Manual, sometimes called the Employee Handbook, is an extremely important tool that must absolutely be in place and properly used to protect you, the owner of the business. I cannot tell you how many lawsuits have been lost because the company's policies were either not clearly or legally spelled out, or not consistently enforced. Here's a general outline of how your CPM should be laid out:

1. Welcome: Congratulate the employee for being selected by the company and let them know that they were selected because company management believes they bring the attributes necessary to support the mission of the company.

2. Company History and Ownership: It's amazing how many employees don't know who they're working for. Tell them who you are and about your company. Make a commitment to meet them and follow through.

3. Company Mission Statement: You created your mission statement when you built your business plan. In your policy manual, you want to convey it to your employees. Focus on your commitment to great guest service, high quality food and drink, and a healthy company culture.

4. Organizational Chart: Many companies fail to tell their employees the organization's management structure. Since it will tend to change, this is an area that will need to be updated as the structure changes. You've told them who owns the company, and they probably have met the specific manager they'll be working with. But tell them who runs the office and other departments of the organization so they recognize that your company is a well-oiled machine and they will recognize other members of the management team as they meet them.

5. Equal Opportunity Employer (EOE): Make it clear in your policy manual that your are committed to comply with Title VII of the Civil Rights Act and will not discriminate based on race, religious beliefs, color, national origin, physical or mental handicap, age, gender, or marital status. There are many online resources in this area and your state's labor department will also provide guidance in the wording you use.

6. Employment "At Will": Many states are considered "at will" to some degree. It's important that you know what your state's position is on this issue. "At Will" means that an employee may be terminated by an employer "at their will," just as the employee can quit at any time at their will. Most "At Will" states allow termination without explanation or cause. However, some states require an explanation and even dictate what parameters that explanation can fall under. Some states dictate that "At Will Employment" is permitted during a probationary period of a certain amount of time. Claims of wrongful termination are rampant and employers that clearly spell out policies in the manual are more likely to win a lawsuit or have one dismissed.

7. "Open Door" Communication: I recommend a statement in your policy manual that you have an "Open Door" communication policy. This allows employees who have a grievance that they can't resolve with their immediate manager to comfortably go to the next level, ultimately even to the ownership. Your managers must be clear about this policy and support it. Many grievances can be resolved in objective and practical ways through this approach.

8. General Communication: Make sure you state how general information will be communicated to employees. This may be on a bulletin board where memos may be posted, notes on paychecks, or through messages through the POS system or timekeeping system. There are certain posters that are required to be posted in areas accessible to all employees such as state and federal labor laws, OSHA requirements, etc. Be sure to tell your employees where this information is found in your policy manual.

9. Sexual Harassment, Zero Tolerance: State very clearly that you are serious about your company's culture prohibiting sexual harassment. Define sexual harassment and make sure that employees are clear what is meant by the term "hostile work place." Tell them up front that such things as obscene jokes, sexual advances, and even flirtatious behavior can be construed as sexual harassment. Commit to them that management will address any and all claims of sexual harassment, but can't do so if they don't know about it.

10. Compensation: Make sure employees know what their starting wage is. Tell them how the pay periods work and when they can

pick up paychecks. Discuss any programs that are in place such as certifications that can lead to wage increases. State that merit increases are at the discretion of management. Discuss benefit programs that may be in place such as health insurance allowances, discounted meals, etc.

11. Rules and Regulations: Cover everything, including but not limited to the following:
    - schedule requests and breaks
    - Uniform policy, dress code, personal hygiene, acceptable jewelry, etc.
    - injuries—both employee and customer, and how they should be handled
    - employee parking
    - employee visitors
    - advances on pay
    - use of phone/cell phones on duty

12. Discipline: Discuss your system of discipline. Here you can list "Prohibited Conduct" that may lead to immediate termination, such as theft, harassment of employees or customers, insubordination, etc. Discuss the various levels of discipline that management may use, including verbal warnings, written warnings, suspension, and termination.

13. Conclusion: Conclude by commenting that every employee is a member of the "public relations team." Commit to answer any and all questions that employees may have. State that the Policy Manual is always available to them for review.

14. Employee Acknowledgement Form: Have each employee sign a statement that they have read and understand the Policy Manual, and place it in their file with other employment related information such as their application, W-4, I-9, certification tests, uniform agreement, etc.

EMPLOYEE OPERATIONS MANUAL (EOM)

The EOM is really the "how to" manual for all non-management positions. It is a written documentation of each job position, with a general description of the job and the job responsibilities. Here are the sections that I recommend for the Employee Operations Manual:

I. New Employee Orientation

Each and every employee should go through this process. It is appropriate to conduct orientation in groups or individually. It should be conducted by a member of the management team and should follow this general approach:

1. Show the new employee how to clock in. That means that a well-prepared training manager has set them up in the timekeeping system in advance.

2. Have them read through the Employee Policy Manual. Then the training manager should review the Manual with them and answer any questions they have. Special emphasis should be placed on such sections as compensation (make sure they know when their first paycheck will be issued), schedule requests, employee injury reporting, harassment, and discipline.

3. Take care of the paperwork; this will include the employee signing Policy Manual acknowledgement, uniform agreement, and required federal forms such as W-4, I-9, etc.

4. Issue their uniform if applicable, and allow them to change into it in privacy.

5. Then, give them a tour of your business. Show them where to find employee lockers, employee restrooms, the office, and all the production areas of your operation. Introduce them to your crew and other management team members. Show them where a first aid kit is and the location of fire extinguishers. Show them where they find MSDS (Material Safety Data Sheets) information. Note: MSDS information must be readily accessible in compliance with federal OSHA requirements. Employees must know what an MSDS is, and where to find them. Show them where they can find labor law posters and how they can access company communications.

6. Finally, administer a rudimentary "employee orientation test" that reviews key points in the Policy Manual and other information they've received during the orientation. Grade the test, review any questions that they missed, and put the test in their employee file.

7. Discuss their training schedule/strategy with them.

They are now ready to go on to their specific position training and you have just ensured that you have a strong defense against any future claim that they might make against you.

II. Food Safety and Handling Practices

I recommend that every employee get some degree of formal training in food safety and handling practices. Some local municipalities require that food handlers take a course through the local health department, and be issued a food handler's card. Other municipalities may offer it on a voluntary basis. Either way, participating in these programs is a good idea and helps to put you in the good graces of the local health department.

Food safety is a practice that every restaurant or food facility must closely adhere to. The following comes right out of the health department manual and is information I've used in franchises that I've owned and helped to develop.

At some time during our lives we will all get food poisoning. Foodborne Illness (FBI) is a disease that is transmitted to people by the food they eat, and can range from mild to severe. If we have a mild case, we may feel as though we have the flu and suffer symptoms such as an elevated temperature, vomiting, and diarrhea, which may dissipate in a few hours or continue for several days. Some cases can be so severe they require hospitalization, and the most severe episodes can result in death. Even a mild case of food poisoning is an uncomfortable experience that all of us would like to avoid.

A single outbreak of Foodborne Illness is not only devastating to the person who gets sick but can damage the company as well. Some of the costs associated with food poisoning can be an increase in insurance, loss of customer sales, embarrassing news stories, a damaged reputation, and lawsuits. It is your job to ensure your guests receive the safest, highest quality food on the market. Foodborne Illness is 100% avoidable with some very simple and easy food handling procedures.

Some of the most common causes of Foodborne Illness are:

1. TIME/TEMPERATURE ABUSE: Caused by failure to cook, cool, and hold foods to specified time and temperatures.

2. POOR PERSONAL HYGIENE: Caused by failure to wash hands properly or frequently, team members who work when they are ill, and team members who improperly treat and/or cover cuts, scratches or boils.

3. CROSS-CONTAMINATION: Caused by transfer of harmful microorganisms from one food/food surface to another, failure to clean and sanitize food-contact surfaces properly, and allowing raw food to touch or drip onto fully cooked, ready-to-eat food.

There are three types of FOOD HAZARDS:

- Biological: microorganisms
- Physical: foreign objects in food
- Chemical: cleaning supplies, pesticides, and toxins

BIOLOGICAL HAZARDS

Biological hazards can be divided into four groups:

- Bacteria
- Viruses
- Parasites
- Fungi

Some foods come to us with biological hazards already present (raw beef may contain e-coli); Hepatitis A and Staph can be carried by people; Listeria and Bacillius Cereus are found in the air or soil. Food is contaminated when the level of these hazards reaches unsafe proportions. Subsequently, if people eat this food, they may become ill.

BACTERIA

The most common biological hazard is bacteria. Bacteria grows best under six conditions known by the acronym FATTOM:

- Food
- Acidity
- Temperature
- Time
- Oxygen
- Moisture

FOOD: Like all living things, bacteria needs food to grow. Bacteria love food that is high in protein and carbohydrates, for example, meat, poultry, dairy products, and eggs.

ACIDITY: Foods that are neutral or slightly acidic (PH between 4.6 and 7.5) support rapid bacteria growth.

TEMPERATURE: The Temperature Danger Zone is 40° F to 140° F. When food is kept outside of this zone, it slows the growth of bacteria, but does not kill the bacteria.

TIME: Under the right conditions, bacteria can double every twenty minutes. Food should not remain in the Temperature Danger Zone for more than four hours. Do not ever use food past its expiration date.

OXYGEN: Some bacteria need oxygen to grow.

MOISTURE: Bacteria grow best in high-moisture foods. We measure the moisture content of food with a water activity test. Potentially hazardous food has a water activity of above .85.

Common types of bacteria include but are not limited to:

- E. COLI 0157: found in beef
- SALMONELLA: most commonly found in poultry, eggs and soil
- STAPH: comes from people

It is important to remember that all these bacteria can be controlled or killed by:

- Cooking all products to the temperatures and times specified in the recipe.
- In addition to heating food to the proper temperatures, we must make sure we don't cross-contaminate cooked food (ready-to-eat) with raw food. Maintain a safe zone of separation between raw and cooked foods.
- Wash, rinse, and sanitize all cutting boards, food contact surfaces, and equipment between product changes.
- Practice good personal hygiene, especially hand washing.
- Make sure you properly cover cuts and sores with a bandage and a clean disposable glove.

PHYSICAL HAZARDS

Physical hazards are foreign objects in food. Some common physical hazards are:

- Metal shavings from a can opener, scrub pads, or other cleaning utensils.
- Staples, twist ties, or plastic clips from packaging.
- Bandages should be covered with a clean, disposable glove.
- Hair must be restrained in a cap.
- Dirt or debris in the produce.

CHEMICAL HAZARDS

Chemical hazards can include toxic metals, cleaning solutions, and pesticides. Some common chemical hazards are:

- Toxins from lead, copper, and brass. This is why it is important to only use food-grade equipment and utensils that are purchased from an approved supplier.
- Chemicals like cleaning products, polishes, lubricants, sanitizers, and bleach must be labeled and stored separately from all food.
- Pesticides can be found on unwashed vegetables.

Most of these potential problems can be eliminated with proper handling procedures. If we all take the proper steps we can stop Foodborne Illness before it starts.

THERMOMETERS

Thermometers are our best tools for fighting Foodborne Illness. Always use thermometers that can be calibrated daily in the restaurant. It is important to remember that dropping or bumping a thermometer can cause it to fall out of calibration, and it may, therefore, need to be recalibrated during your shift.

STEPS TO CALIBRATING THERMOMETERS

1. Fill a glass with ice. Add tap water until the glass is full. Stir for twenty seconds.
2. Place the thermometer stem in the ice water, making sure the sensing area is submerged. Do not let the stem touch the bottom or sides of the glass. Holding the thermometer from the dial, wait forty seconds.
3. Read the thermometer. It should be 32° F.

4. If the temperature doesn't say 32° F follow these steps:

   – While holding the thermometer in the ice water
   – Rotate the adjusting nut with a small wrench until the temperature reads 32° F.

GUIDELINES FOR TEMPING FOOD

- Always take two temperatures from different locations of the product; both readings must be within the proper temperature specification.
- Do not let the thermometer touch the sides or bottom of the pan.
- Insert the thermometer at least halfway into the thickest part of the food.
- Wait until the temperature stabilizes before taking the reading.

- Always wash with soap, rinse, and sanitize the thermometer after each use.
- Place the thermometer back in its case or sleeve after each use.

Two of the leading causes of Foodborne Illness are:

1. Temperature Abuse
2. Cross-Contamination

It is easy for food to fall into the Temperature Danger Zone when it is being prepared and cooked because that's when it's out of the proper storage area the longest, and being handled the most.

PREVENTION OF TEMPERATURE ABUSE

- Have calibrated thermometers clean and ready to use.
- Only remove the amount of food you have time to work on. For example, if you are prepping beef for the FWE Cook and Hold only pull out the amount stated on your prep sheet.
- Make sure the recipe is in front of you. Follow recipes exactly to ensure food is prepared and cooked properly.
- Gather all utensils and other equipment you may need before you remove food from the freezer or cooler.
- Return foods to the cooler or freezer as quickly as possible after preparation is complete.
- Ensure all cooking equipment is working properly.

PREVENTION OF CROSS-CONTAMINATION

- Prepare raw meats in an area away from any other products that have been cooked or are ready to eat.
- Wash all whole fruits and vegetables in the veggie wash sink.
- Use separate cutting boards and utensils for different foods where the recipe indicates.
- Ensure team members wash hands between tasks, job position changes, and especially after handling raw meat or fish. Gloves do not take the place of hand washing.
- Gloves must be worn when handling raw meat or fish.
- Change aprons after handling raw meat or fish. Change aprons throughout your shift as needed when the aprons becomes dirty.
- Sanitizer buckets must be changed every two hours. Use a designated sanitizer bucket for raw meat and fish clean-up only.

PROPER THAWING GUIDELINES

- Thaw food in the walk-in, never at room temperature. Thawing food should be placed in a hotel pan or Cambro on the bottom rack of the walk-in so it doesn't drip on the food below it. The food must be marked with the date it was taken out of the freezer for thawing.
- Foods should be completely thawed before cooking (unless the recipe states otherwise).
- In an emergency, if you need to thaw a product faster than the above process allows, you can place the food in a bowl in an empty sink and let COLD water run over the top of the product. Make sure the water is cold and easily flows down the drain. Never use hot water.

COOKING AND COOLING TIMES AND TEMPERATURES

Because food contains bacteria, which causes food poisoning, other areas of concern are cooking, chilling, and holding products at proper temperature. It is imperative that meats are cooked to temperature and held at that temperature for a specified amount of time to sufficiently kill the bacteria. Vegetables must be washed with a veggie wash solution to clean the surface of debris and pesticide residue. Products held on the hot line must maintain certain temperatures, as must cold products being held under refrigeration. When we need to cool food for storage, it must be cooled to a designated temperature within a specified amount of time. When all of these steps and procedures are followed, we can eliminate food poisoning. Refer to the chart below for proper cooking times and temperatures.

A few important reminders about cooking:

- Always follow the recipes.
- Check temperatures in the thickest part of the food.
- Temperature, not time, is always the final determinate in cooking.
- Always reheat to 165° F for fifteen seconds.

Prep personnel, managers, and anyone working in the kitchen or on the service line must have proper cooking times memorized and follow procedures at all times.

COOLING

The longer it takes to cool a product, the more opportunity bacteria have to grow. This is why cooling needs to happen rapidly! There are never any exceptions to this rule.

Cool food from 140° F to 70° F in two hours or less, and from 70° F to 40° F in four hours or less.

Cooling Guidelines:

- Do not cool food in plastic containers. Aluminum or stainless steel pans conduct heat away from the food more effectively.
- Cut large foods into smaller portions to cool faster.
- Place food to be cooled in a shallow layer to cool faster.
- Place food to be cooled on the top shelf of the walk-in where air can circulate over the product, cooling it faster.
- Never use the reach-in or under-the-counter refrigerators to cool food.
- Stir foods often during the cooling process.

PERSONAL HYGIENE

Food is exposed to team members many times during its process through the restaurant. Because we come in contact with the food so many times before it reaches the guest, we can easily contaminate the food. It is important to understand how food handlers can contaminate food so we can take steps to avoid contamination. Be aware of food handlers who:

- Have an illness like Hepatitis A or Salmonellas
- Have infected cuts, or injuries that are not properly treated and covered
- Have a gastrointestinal illness
- Live with or are exposed to someone who is ill
- Touch something that contaminates their hands and do not wash properly

Simple personal acts can contaminate food, like:

- Touching the hair or scalp
- Coughing or sneezing into the hand
- Nose picking
- Rubbing an ear
- Scratching the face or other body part
- Touching a pimple or open sore
- Spitting

Team Members must pay close attention to everything they touch, and wash their hands often and properly. This section will cover four practices of good personal hygiene:

1. Hand washing
2. Glove use
3. Proper uniform and personal appearance
4. Reporting illness and injury

First and foremost, WASH YOUR HANDS! This is the most common way to avoid Foodborne Illnesses. You should wash your hands at least every twenty minutes! It is important to wash your hands if you:

- Sneeze or cough
- Blow your nose
- Touch your face or hair
- Take out the trash
- Take a break
- Clean the dining room
- Change job positions
- Handle money
- Use the restroom

In addition to washing your hands in the restroom, you will also wash your hands in the kitchen before returning to your workstation. Even though you washed your hands in the bathroom, on your way back to your station, you had to open doors and touch other areas of the restaurant that the public has also touched. There is no way to know if the previous person who touched that area washed his hands. Therefore, it is good practice to wash your hands again when you return to your workstation. It is also important for the public to see you washing your hands. The guests don't know for sure that you washed your hands just before leaving the bathroom, therefore, this allows the public to see employees frequently washing their hands, which shows that we take pride in personal hygiene.

The restaurant is equipped with designated hand washing sinks. These sinks are used only for hand washing and must have:

- Antibacterial hand soap
- Hot running water

- One-use disposable towels
- A waste basket

HAND WASHING PROCEDURE

- Turn on the water as hot as you can comfortably stand it (110° F) and wet your hands.
- Apply antibacterial soap.
- Rub hands together, scrub up to the elbows for a minimum of twenty seconds.
- Clean under your nails and between your fingers.
- Dry hands and turn off the water using the towel, not your hands.
- Use the towel to open any door you may encounter between the bathroom and your workstation.

Hand Maintenance Guidelines:

- Fingernails should be kept short and clean.
- Team members who handle food cannot wear fingernail polish or false nails.
- The only jewelry allowed is two studs per ear.
- Cuts or injures must be cleaned, treated, bandaged, and covered with a finger cot or glove.

Gloves are a good way to prevent contamination but should never be used in place of good hand washing. Gloves will be readily available and for one use only.

Glove Guidelines—Team Members must wear gloves when:

- Handling raw meat or fish
- Handling ready-to-eat foods that will not be cooked any further
- They have a cut or injury on their hand or fingers. Wash hands before putting on the gloves. Change gloves frequently, as often as you would wash your hands.

REPORTING ILLNESS AND INJURY

Team members must report health problems to their manager before working with food. They must also immediately tell their manager if they become ill or injured during their shift. In addition, managers must prohibit team members from working if they have any of the following symptoms:

- Fever
- Diarrhea
- Vomiting
- Sore Throat
- Jaundice
- Achy
- Nausea

Good personal hygiene habits do not just happen. They must be trained and receive constant follow-up by the manager. The single most effective thing a manager can do is lead by example.

MANAGERS MUST

- Wash their hands every twenty minutes
- Have a perfect uniform at all times
- Exhibit excellent grooming habits
- Hold all team members to the same high standard

Make it easy for the team members to practice good personal hygiene by keeping the hand washing areas stocked, in good repair, and accessible. Have clean aprons available. Make sure there are plenty of opened boxes of gloves in key areas, such as the prep station and the service line.

FOLLOW UP

Leading by example, training, and ease of use will not be complete without follow-up.

- Address any personal hygiene issues immediately.
- Set clear expectations during orientation and training. This will make follow-up easier when it's necessary.
- Focus on the issue and consequence, not the person. This will make addressing issues such as body odor or personal habits much easier.
- Use positive reinforcement. Praise employees when you see them practicing good personal hygiene habits.

CLEANING AND SANITIZING

Keeping the restaurant clean will help prevent Foodborne Illness and ensure we present the best possible image to our guests. A clean restaurant and clean equipment will also:

- Lower maintenance costs
- Last longer
- Be easier to clean
- Be a pleasant place to work
- Discourage pests from living and breeding in the restaurant
- Instill pride in your crew

What is the difference between cleaning and sanitizing? Cleaning is the process of removing visible food or debris. Sanitizing is the process of reducing harmful microorganisms to a safe level. Items must be cleaned and rinsed before being sanitized.

All food contact surfaces must be kept cleaned and sanitized. A food contact surface is anything that comes in contact or may come in contact, with food.

This includes:

- Cooking utensils
- Prep tables
- Pans, Cambros, lexans, and lids
- Cutting boards
- Knives
- All surfaces of cooking equipment
- Serving trays
- Any shelving or bins that hold these items
- Thermometers

Food contact surfaces must be cleaned:

- After each use
- When you begin working with another type of food
- Any time your work is interrupted
- Any time these items become contaminated
- At four hour intervals if the items are being continually used (such as cutting boards or knives)

CHEMICAL SAFETY GUIDELINES

- Use only food safe approved sanitizers.
- Store all cleaning products in approved areas away from all food and heat sources.

- Store chemicals in their original containers or properly labeled bottles.
- Never mix chemicals together.
- Use only the appropriate chemical for the job. For example, don't use floor cleaner to clean the prep tables.
- Avoid contamination of food. Cover food or spray chemicals on a towel away from food.
- Test the strength of the sanitizer in the 3/4 compartment sink every two hours.

SANITIZER BUCKETS

In addition to regular cleaning and sanitizing of food contact surfaces, we must also have sanitizer buckets on hand. These are used to clean-as-you-go, wiping up spills and keeping things clean between regular washing and sanitizing.

Sanitizer buckets should be located at all workstations and be set up as the station is opened.

- At several locations on the serving line
- In the prep area
- In the kitchen

TO SET UP SANITIZER BUCKETS

1. Properly set up the sanitizer compartment of the sink.
2. Test the water with sanitizer strip (a chemically treated strip of paper that indicates by the color that the mixture is correct).
3. Fill each bucket half full with the water from the sanitizer sink.
4. Place a clean towel in each bucket.
5. Place the buckets at their station.

If, during Step 2, the mixture in the sink is incorrect, contact the chemical company to make the proper adjustments the dispenser.

CHANGE SANITIZER BUCKETS

- When the sanitizer level falls below 220 PPM. You can find this out by testing with a test strip.
- When the water becomes soiled
- Every two hours

CLEANING PROCEDURES

There are three main types of cleaning procedures:

- Clean-as-you-go
- Dishwashing
- Clean-in-place

CLEAN-AS-YOU-GO:

Clean-as-you-go is the practice of keeping things clean all day long. Not only will this help to give the restaurant a clean appearance, it will make end of the shift clean-up easier, reduce bacteria, and make a more enjoyable place to work.

Clean-as-you-go practices:

- Sweep and mop floors at regular intervals
- Clean up spills as soon as they happen
- Continuously wipe down food contact surfaces with sanitizer towels
- Replace utensils, serving spoons, and containers as they become dirty
- Wipe down the exterior of equipment whenever there is a few minutes of spare time

DISHWASHING

FOLLOW SPECIFIC INSTRUCTIONS FOR SET-UP, USAGE, CLOSING, AND CLEANING THE DISH MACHINE.

GENERAL DISWASHING GUIDELINES FOR THREE-COMPARTMENT SINK

- Never place sharp knives or blades into the dishwater. Wash them yourself and store them in the proper place.
- Always pre-scrape and pre-spray items.
- Pre-rinse all items that have come in contact with food.

SETTING UP THE THREE-COMPARTMENT SINK FOR POTS AND PANS

Each basin must be set up according to these guidelines in order to make the whole system works. Before you set up the sinks, make sure each basin and drain board are clean and ready to be used. The three sinks are for washing, rinsing, and sanitizing. Some states require four-compartment sinks. If your restaurant is equipped with a four-compartment sink, you will have a pre-scrape/spray area. This is used to remove loose soil, food, and microorganisms. This will extend the life of the wash water and make cleaning easier. Clean this area as food and debris accumulate.

- The first basin is the WASH basin, containing soap. Fill the basin with 80° F to 120° F water to the fill line. Soak items first to make cleaning easier. Using a brush, towel, or scrub pad, remove all visible food and soil. Items should be immersed for at least three minutes. This basin needs to be changed when the temperature drops below 80° F or the water becomes dirty.
- The second basin is for RINSING the soap and other debris off the item. This sink is also filled with water 80° F to 120° F. This basin must be changed when the water becomes dirty or soapy. Soap reduces the effectiveness of sanitizer.
- The third basin is the SANITIZER sink. This sink gets filled with water 70° F to 75° F. Items should be immersed for three minutes. This sink needs to have 220 PPM of sanitizer to be used effectively. This compartment must be changed when the water becomes dirty, when the test strip indicates the PPM has fallen below 200, or when the water temperature falls below 75° F.

The drain board must be cleaned and sanitized before using. Allow items that have just been washed to air dry on the drain board. Do not nest items. Allow all items to dry completely before storing. Clean and sanitize the drain board every time the sanitizer sink is changed.

CLEAN-IN-PLACE EQUIPMENT

All equipment must be kept clean and all food contact surfaces must be cleaned and sanitized. Because most equipment cannot be placed in the dishwasher machine or the dishwashing sink, it is called clean-in-place.

Examples of clean-in-place equipment are:

- Meat Slicer
- Mixers
- Under-the-counter refrigerators

In general, follow these steps for clean-in-place equipment:

- Turn off and unplug equipment.
- Remove loose food and soil from surfaces.

- Remove loose food and soil from under and around equipment.
- Remove detachable parts and wash, rinse, and sanitize at the 3- or 4-compartment sink.
- Wash surface with approved cleaners and cleaning towel.
- Rinse surfaces using a bucket of clean water and cleaning towel.
- Sanitize surfaces by spraying with a bottle of sanitizer.
- Air-dry all parts before reassembling and plugging the back in.

III. Job Descriptions

Each job position should have a section in the EOM describing the job. The following is a recommended format for each job description:

- Job Purpose: State an overview of the job. For example, for a server: "To provide prompt and friendly service to the restaurant's guests."
- Job Scope: This is a more detailed description of what the job encompasses. For example, for a server: "Handle an assigned station of five tables, including taking drink and food orders, delivering the orders, clearing the tables, and closing the check."
- Job Objective: Describe the expected outcome of the job position. For example, for a server: "To ensure a high quality of service and guests that are fully satisfied with their dining experience."
- Job Responsibilities: A detailed description of the required tasks of the job. For example, for a server: "Opening the station and opening side work, greeting guests, taking orders, delivering food and beverage, checking the table, clearing the table, building check average with desserts and bar drinks, closing checks, closing side work, check-out."

Job descriptions should be reviewed with the training manager as a prerequisite to the employee's continued on-the-job training. They can be as general or detailed as you see fit. Most learning will occur as employees work with a trainer, following them through the actual process of performing the job. However, the EOM is a resource for employees and establishes a written guideline for each job position.

FINANCIAL REQUIREMENTS

Below is a general list of pre-opening start-up costs. Please note that no operational costs are included.

1. Lease Cost: Lease cost is your monthly rent, assuming you have signed a lease with a property owner and don't own the property yourself. Remember, *your rent must be no more than 10% of your sales.*

2. Normal Leases: Normal leases will require the first month's rent in advance.

3. Security Deposit: Security deposits will normally be one month's payment to be applied to the last month of the lease.

4. Tenant Finishing Costs: Tenant finishing costs will vary greatly depending on your concept. Generally, your square footage build-out cost will run from $100 psf (per square foot) to $150 psf, depending on your concept. Tenant finish cost will vary according to your décor and geographic location. You, of course, will want to get bids from contractors. I recommend that you use only a contractor who specializes in restaurants. Additionally, I recommend that you get at least three construction bids from different contractors. By having three bids, a high, low, and third bid, you will have an idea which contractor's bid is more realistic and accurate. A bid that is too low can be as bad as one that is too high. If too low, something obviously has been forgotten.

5. Miscellaneous Expenses: These will vary from county to county and state to state. You can get estimates on these costs by calling City Hall and your local building department.

6. Furniture, Fixtures, and Equipment (FF&E): Your FF&E cost will also correspond to your restaurant concept. It can easily range from $100,000 to $300,000, depending on how simple or elaborate your concept might be. I do not recommend buying used equipment; certainly not without warranties on the equipment. Be especially careful about equipment that has a motor, generator, or compressor component. It is almost impossible to tell how effective or how long used equipment will last.

7. Signage: Signage costs will vary according to the size and number of signs that you require. You can get estimates from local sign companies.

8. Opening Food Inventory and Supplies: These costs will vary with your menu and concept. You can get deliveries from your vendors two to three times a week, so there is no need to carry a large inventory, especially on perishables.

9. Computer Hardware and Software: These can range from $5,000 and up, depending on the restaurant concept, how elaborate you want your reporting to be, and the size of your operations. Research this area carefully. There are restaurant POS systems that will vary greatly in cost. It's a lot like buying a new car; many of the extra bells and whistles may look good, but they may not be necessary. Buy only what you need. Many of the well-known POS systems are nothing more than over-kill. Review what they offer with your accountant and choose what best fits your accounting and security needs.

10. Grand Opening: An effective grand opening can be achieved for around $5,000.

11. Professional Fees: These fees generally refer to legal and account- ing costs. Budget enough for your attorney to negotiate a Letter of Intent, which should precede your lease, and then to review the lease. You will need accounting services to set up your charge of accounts and bookkeeping system.

12. Triple Net Costs: If you are in an "in line" location, like a strip center, your landlord will carry the building insurance. The insur- ance charges will be part of Triple Net charges that will be in addition to your rent. Typically, Triple Net charges will cover building insurance, property taxes, and common area mainte- nance. You will pay your proportionate share of the Triple Net charges based on the center's square footage versus your aggre- gate amount of square footage leased.

13. Insurance Costs: Additionally, your restaurant will need to carry a substantial liability insurance policy. (For all legal or accounting advice, contact an attorney or CPA who specializes in setting up small businesses.)

Have your attorney draft a penalty clause in your construction contract. Your restaurant lease will have a time factor for construc- tion, which will correspond to when you begin paying rent. The pen- alty amount should be at least the same as your rent would be for each month the construction is not completed on time.

INTERIOR FLOOR PLANS AND ELEVATIONS

For your floor plan, you will need advice from a knowledgeable restaurant professional. There are consulting companies and architectural firms that provide this service and the restaurant equipment company that you select may also provide the needed services. Of course, if you are buying into a franchise, both floor plan and equipment specifications are part of the package you get from the franchise company.

If you intend to lease an existing space, you will need to get the landlord to provide you with "as built" plans of the space you're leasing. Your architect, or the franchise company's architect, will need this plan so they can design your restaurant's floor plan and layout. If you are not buying a franchise, be careful when choosing your architect. He or she may not specialize in restaurants and may not be qualified to specify the proper equipment you need to create your menu items, or design the proper space/kitchen layout. My advice is to hire a knowledgeable consultant who can tell you exactly what layout and equipment you will need for your concept and menu. The salesman from whom you're buying the equipment is just that—a salesman—normally driven by a profit motive. Additionally, while most equipment salesmen have knowledge of their equipment, they are not as qualified as an experienced consultant in selecting the best equipment for your specific needs.

Your rent is predicated on the restaurant's square footage. A significant percentage of your operating costs go to rent, which is calculated by sales-per-seat. Therefore, you want to reap the highest possible profit out of every square foot. The technological advances in the restaurant industry have been significant in the last few years. There is new equipment available today that not only is smaller, but fully capable of performing multi-functions that normally would take several pieces of equipment to accomplish. There is also equipment available that cuts preparation time in half, thus reducing labor costs and increasing efficiency. Walk-in refrigeration and storage historically took a great deal of back-of-the-house space. New and improved shelving equipment and storage techniques will save on space and improve efficiency of the kitchen and staff.

Be on your guard when buying used equipment, especially any equipment that has a compressor or motor. There is no tried and true method that reveals wear and tear on compressors or motor-driven equipment. The outside can clean up nicely, but the inside may be ready to burn out. Make sure you get a history of use, but understand that even then there is no guarantee the equipment has been properly maintained. Stainless steel tables are normally okay, as long as they are the right size and fit your kitchen layout. Remember, an efficient kitchen is a production line, where each part must fit like a glove in order to function properly.

Fuel efficiency is an increasingly important factor in cost control. Energy-efficient equipment is one aspect of controlling costs, though energy savings should go beyond equipment, and include systems for the entire restaurant. Your equipment consultant, architect, and contractor should be encouraged to think "green."

New restaurant construction is becoming considerably less attractive due to rising real estate and construction costs, which have been rising at a double-digit rate for years. This is responsible for square foot ROI (return on investment) rates to decline. Additionally, in many areas, neighborhood activism (NIMBY: not in my back yard) has caused increasingly restrictive compliance demands, further adding to the cost and construction time. In many cases, the added value of your own building is questionable because of the excess capital required, and substandard returns.

Viable options to single purpose new construction include conversions of existing retail space, or taking over a closed-down restaurant. Significant cost savings can be realized if, for example, the necessary electrical power and panels are in place. HVAC can be a major cost. A typical restaurant kitchen will require the electrical requirements of a 3-phase, 400 amp service. HVAC requirements vary geographically, but on average would be one ton per two hundred square feet of restaurant space.

Probably the most cost-effective way of building your restaurant is by converting an existing restaurant. In addition to a significant savings in construction costs, another advantage is that the previous business can give you some estimate of the location's potential for success.

However, taking over a failed restaurant can be a two-sided sword: If the previous restaurant in the location failed, make sure you have a good handle on the reasons why. Assure yourself the failure was not *due to the location.* Use the same site evaluation of traffic counts and demographics for an existing location as you would for a new site location.

Most architects will provide you with an elevation rendering. The floor plan can be in black and white, but renderings should be done in color. Remember, if you are planning on getting financial help, you will be using this business plan document as a primary sales tool.

I cannot emphasize the importance of pre-planning your restaurant kitchen design. How critical is this area for success? The following is from direct experience: As mentioned before, a former partner and I owned and operated a restaurant consulting business. One day, several years ago, I received a call from a gentleman in Florida. He told us he had a bagel restaurant that was doing great business, but he wasn't making any money! I suggested that he send me one of his monthly profit and loss statements. Upon reviewing his P&L statement, the problem was immediately apparent. His monthly labor cost was approximately 20% higher than it should have been, and was eating him alive. When I told him this, he acknowledged he was aware of his inflated labor costs, but could not operate his business with fewer people.

At his request, I flew to Florida. Upon entering the restaurant, the problem was readily apparent. There were almost as many employees as there were customers. The owner, who had no previous restaurant experience, had designed the kitchen himself. In many cases, he had the wrong equipment, and in all cases the equipment was laid out incorrectly.

An efficient restaurant kitchen is much like a factory production line: there is a sequence of design that must follow a prescribed plan. Lacking this order of design, a busy kitchen can turn into a Chinese fire drill—mass confusion, with needless overlap of employee roles. The only alternatives for this Florida restaurateur were to continue with profit absorbing labor costs, or shut down long enough to allow remodeling of his kitchen. He chose the latter and, immediately upon reopening, began to turn a profit.

SALES, PROFIT AND LOSS PROJECTIONS

Following is a standard restaurant financial projection format on an Excel spread sheet. You'll see at the beginning that a series of assumptions must be made to build the projection upon. It is here that many an entrepreneur has made the biggest and financially deadliest mistake. Be conservative in your projection. If your restaurant will seat 100 and you think you can turn it over four times a day, do a conservative projection and see how it would look if it turned only two times in a day. You should build three scenarios; Conservative—asking "What if I do half of what I expect to do?"; Realistic—based on your research of similar concepts in similar markets, what you think you'll probably do; and Optimistic—where you really nail it, hit a homerun, etc.

Once those assumptions are made, you can begin to build your projections. The same rule applies to your projected increases in revenue through time. Be conservative! Bankers, investors, and stockholders would rather see you outperform your projections than underperform them. Be sure that you fully understand concepts such as "Return on Investment" and "Internal Rate of Return." If you don't, get advice from your accountants, financial advisors, restaurant association resources, and restaurant operators. Do your homework when it comes to projecting your expenses.

Many new restaurateurs have no idea what their break-even point is. It's a simple equation of understanding what your fixed costs are and adding to it your variable costs. That sum total is your break-even point, that is, the amount of revenue you need to generate in order to cover your costs. Your own compensation may or may not be in it. I recommend you put it in as a fixed cost. You may find that it's a lot more difficult to cover your debt when you're paying yourself. But if you can't pay yourself, why do it all?

While the following spreadsheet template shows a monthly breakdown, it is more important to look at a projection over the first two to five years. How will rent increases or interest rate increases impact your profitability? What will property taxes be doing in the next few years? What about legislation that impacts your labor cost, such as minimum wage increases or mandatory healthcare taxes. In other words, look forward with a realistic view that expenses will be rising and have a plan to address that reality.

I've often noted that, for some reason, many people who enter the restaurant business neglect to fully educate themselves about the numbers. Understanding your Profit and Loss statements is the key to maximizing profits. In addition to your accountant's advice, bringing in an experienced consultant to review your P&L statements once a month, for the first six months you're in business, is an excellent (and profitable!) idea.

SALES AND OPERATING INCOME PROJECTIONS – Year 1

Assumptions:

SALES

	$	
	a	
	$	

x Average # of customers/day
+ Total avg. Daily Sales

Increase per increased sales & operating/mo.
Increase per increased parts/mo.
Min # cust sales to breakeven sales

FIXED COSTS
Labor, salaried
Rent/CAM
Property Taxes (NN% Report)
Insurance
Interest on debt
Other fixed costs

VARIABLE COSTS

Food Cost	$ xxxxx	% of food sales
Beverage Cost	$ xxxxx	% of beverage sales
Labor, hourly	$ xxxxx	% of total sales
Payroll taxes	$ xxxxx	% of payroll
Worker's Comp.	$ xxxxx	% of payroll
Repair/Maint.	$ xxxxx	% of total sales
Supplies		% of total sales
Marketing		% of total sales
Utilities		% of total sales
Administrative		% of total sales
Other operating exp.		% of total sales

Operating Income Pro-forma:

	JAN	FEB	MAR	APR	MAY	JUN	JUL	AUG	SEP	OCT	NOV	DEC
INCOME												
Food Sales												
Beverage Sales												
TOTAL SALES												
Other Income												
TOTAL INCOME												
EXPENSES												
Food Cost												
Beverage Cost												
COST OF GOODS												
Labor - Salaried												
Labor - Hourly												
Pay.ll taxes												
Worker's Comp.												
PAYROLL COST												
Repair & Maint.												
Supplies												
Marketing/Advert.												
Utilities												
Admin. Exp.												
Interest Exp.												
Other Exp.												
OPERATING EXP.												
OPERATING INCOME												

Section IV:
Conclusion

At the time of this writing, I have been in the restaurant business as an owner/operator, franchisor, or consultant for over fifty years. My career has spanned many different restaurant concepts, from basic, family style to new age disco night clubs. I have run the gamut, from fine dining to fast-casual; and, in spite of the challenges that often arose, I enjoyed every minute of it.

Developing a new concept, no matter what the category of restaurant, is a simple process of following the tried and true basic ideas. Everything remains the same, except for the menu, décor, and service system. Your site selection follows those premises we discussed earlier, always being alert to the demographic criteria (who your patrons are) that ultimately defines the success of your concept. Your job descriptions may change, but your operational systems and forms will remain pretty much the same. The smart restaurateur never re-invents the wheel. Once understood, the process is really simple, a whale of a lot of fun, and very fulfilling and rewarding.

The North Woods Inn was my first restaurant as a part owner/manager. From there, I struck out on my own and opened the first Hungry Farmer. Following the Hungry Farmer, I opened the Hungry Dutchman. The Hungry Dutchman was followed by two more Hungry Farmers. Next was the Broker Restaurant in Denver, two PTI (PTI was an acronym that meant nothing and was created to stimulate customer interest in what the name stood for) restaurants in Denver, followed by PTI restaurants in Dallas, Houston, Austin, Cleveland, Arizona, and California. Following a short period of retirement after selling my restaurants, I then opened Wilscam's in downtown Denver. A few years later, I developed a bagel store chain that was to become Einstein Bros. Bagels.

Fortunately, my restaurant career has been mostly successful. However, I must tell you of one spectacular failure. I had sold my restaurants and semi-retired by 1980. The work bug then bit me again, and I felt driven to open a new restaurant. I wanted to try something different, something that would be a real challenge. There was a tremendously popular series on TV during that time called *Dynasty*. The story line dealt with a wealthy oil business family in Denver, and one of the two female leads was Linda Evans, a strikingly beautiful woman. I thought that Linda might welcome a swanky New York type restaurant in Denver.

A healthy dose of ego convinced me to name the restaurant Wilscam's, and it was to be the crème de la crème, no expense spared. The restaurant cost approximately $1 million, a big number in 1980! The dining room was illuminated by crystal chandeliers placed about twenty feet apart, with each chandelier a different color crystal. The ceiling was reflective glass, giving the chandeliers a three-dimensional effect. On one side of the dining room, glass windows faced a small park with flowering trees, which we decorated with tiny pin lights. The reflection of the tree lights outside, and the chandeliers inside, created a spectacular setting. One of the interior walls was a large glass window, affording a view of the bakery inside the kitchen where customers could watch our bakers making croissants, breakfast pastries, and soufflés for dinner.

Waiters and waitress were attired in tuxedos, with white tuxedo shirts and white bow ties. After-dinner drinks were served from a liqueur cart, and coffee was served in a French press at each dining table.

In the center of the lounge area was a large circular marble bar, with cut-glass overhead that reflected pale pink lighting over the bar. The lighting added a touch of glamour and mystery to the bar, and became a great favorite of our customers, both male and female. Helping to enhance the mood was a popular local pianist, who entertained nightly at a baby grand piano.

To get the word out, I contacted all the concierges at the luxurious downtown Denver hotels. When they made reservations at Wilscam's for their guests, we would send a van to transport guests to our restaurant. Of course, the concierge would later receive a nice gratuity.

The menu was Continental Nouvelle, and changed weekly. I spent approximately one year putting together recipes from various cookbooks and food magazines such as *Gourmet, Food and Wine, Savoir, Bon Appetite,* and other magazines noted for their exquisite cuisine. On three by five cards, I divided recipes into categories of appetizers, meat, fowl, fish, game, sauces, vegetables, protein, and desserts. Each Friday, the executive chef, souschef, head baker, managers, and I would gather in my office in front of a large storyboard. We would begin building the following week's menu by selecting and placing on the storyboard four items in each category.

Our location was letter-perfect for our gourmet category restaurant. The Denver Center for Performing Arts complex, made up of nine individual theaters, was located approximately six blocks from the restaurant. The Center featured the best Broadway plays, the Denver Symphony, Denver Ballet and Opera Company, and visiting entertainers. Our comfortable, customized van had seating for twelve, so each evening, we would provide transportation to and from the DCPA for our customers.

The first year we opened, the restaurant was a grand success—*the* place to dine in Denver when you desired a superb gourmet meal—and we were financially successful. However, the second year brought problems not of our own doing. Denver's oil industry suffered a severe downturn, which drastically affected the Denver economy, and the city led the nation in bankruptcies that year. For the next fourteen months, the restaurant lost a significant amount of money. I decided to hang on and try to fix our financial problems. The restaurant had an excellent reputation, but was known to be expensive. I was between a rock and a hard place: no matter what I did internally—short of converting the restaurant to a fast food joint—made little difference, as Denver was in bad straits. I felt like the man in a lake who had an anvil in one hand, and was trying to swim with the other. Friends, even competitors, tried to help, persuading me to "drop the anvil." However, I chose to hang on with both hands and tough it out. Needless to say, the bad Denver economy outlasted me and the restaurant went broke.

The restaurant's failure had a major effect on me and my family, because I had personally guaranteed the lease for twenty years. I had foolishly reasoned that with my experience and previous successes, I could not fail. Big mistake! The obvious lesson here is that the restaurant business is fraught with risk that cannot always be controlled. My advice is to always limit your exposure, and have a viable exit strategy.

Over the years, in addition to owning a national restaurant franchise, my partner and I have been consultants in creating the concepts and opening over ninety restaurants. While I still have ownership in the franchise restaurant company, I am no longer active in it, but continue to work full time as a restaurant consultant.

Quick Rules-of-Thumb:

Following are a few suggestions that I personally feel are imperative to being a successful restaurant entrepreneur:

1. Absentee ownership/management will not work. There are many reasons for this, but most important is the fact that what is important to you is invariably important to your staff. Only you can impart that by your presence and involvement. Your presence will set the tone for your success or your failure.

2. Make sure you are well-financed. A good rule of thumb is to have enough capital to cover the overhead for at least one year. In certain circumstances, it could in fact take that long to begin showing a profit.

3. Surround yourself with the best people available. "Focus on doing the right things, and hire good people to do them right."

4. Volume is the name of the game. Focus on ways to increase volume and your profit will follow accordingly.

5. It takes a special type of personality to be an entrepreneur and be able to sleep at nights knowing that you are financially betting the farm. That is what you must be prepared to do physically, emotionally, and financially. It will take a full commitment of all three to have the best chance for success.

6. To watch the restaurant industry's growth, and to be a part of ever changing market trends, is an ongoing challenge, and exciting to me. Rapidly changing customer demands, based on today's changing lifestyles, requires a constant finger on the pulse of the public and an innovative spirit.

If you remember one thing from this book, here it is. Always start out in the restaurant business with a carefully thought out business plan. If you have been diligent and thoughtful in developing yours, it will spell out exactly what you need to do to if you want to be a success. How important is a business plan, as opposed to just winging it?

Stephen R. Covey, author of the best-selling book *The 7 Habits of Highly Successful People,* states it succinctly: "Failing to plan is planning to fail."

My last bit of advice is probably the most important: *Make sure you are happy in what you are doing!* I firmly believe that a great deal, if not all, of my moderate success can be attributed to the fact that I loved what I was doing. I found personal fulfillment in the restaurant business, and therefore happiness. I enjoyed the creativity it afforded me. To be able to create or be a part of the creation of a restaurant concept can be like creating a beautiful painting, composing music that moves you, or even writing a book. The positive interaction with people can be a rewarding experience. I have made life-long friends with a great many of my co-workers over my years in the industry.

Good luck on your journey, and I hope that you can find that same enjoyment and fulfillment in the restaurant industry that I have found. Enjoy!

CPSIA information can be obtained
at www.ICGtesting.com
Printed in the USA
LVOW07s0651310817
547092LV00001B/60/P

9 781609 119805